W9-BSV-275

PAST LIVES, PRESENT JOY

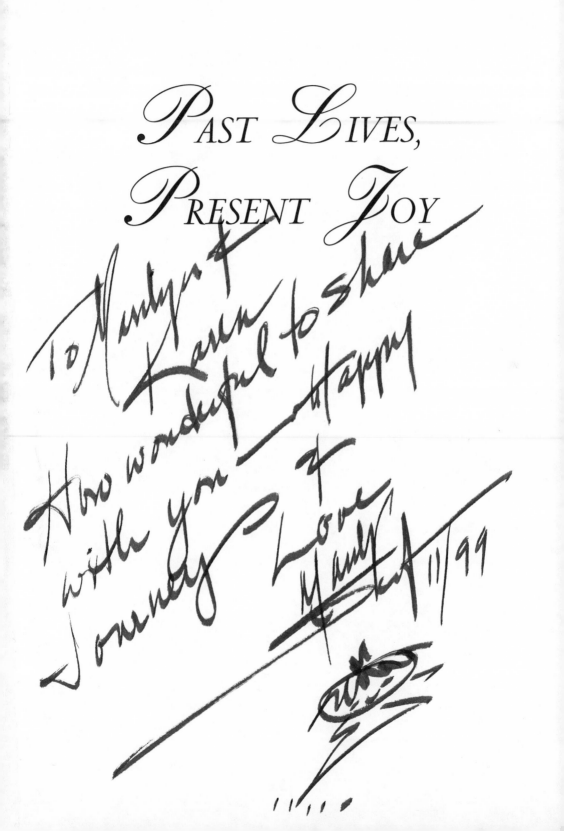

To Marilyn &
Kevin
How wonderful to share
with you Happy
Journey &
Love
Mary [?] 11/99

PAST LIVES, PRESENT JOY

MARILYN C. SUNDERMAN, DFA

Kensington Books
http://www.kensingtonbooks.com

To some of those I've known who are now angels:
Taesoon, Lynn Akana, Joyce Walzak, and especially
to my mom, Josephine Esther Case Sunderman

Also dedicated to my other angels and guides.
I know I did not write this alone; NOW I
know I do not journey alone.

KENSINGTON BOOKS are published by

Kensington Publishing Corp.
850 Third Avenue
New York, NY 10022

Copyright © 1999 by Marilyn C. Sunderman

All rights reserved. No part of this book may be reproduced in any form or by any means without the prior written consent of the Publisher, excepting brief quotes used in reviews.

Kensington and the K logo Reg. U.S. Pat. & TM Off.

Library of Congress Card Catalog Number: 98-066233
ISBN 1-57566-377-5

First Printing: January, 1999
10 9 8 7 6 5 4 3 2 1

Printed in the United States of America

Contents

Acknowledgments

Sometimes there are those who touch your life so specially that you can only softly and humbly whisper a thank you. There are so many of you, more than I can list; please know that your name is written in my special hall of thank yous.

To some of you who held my hand at the edge and led me back: Helen Meyers, Lila and Jerry Ptak, Sherry and Eldon Ploetz, Gary Weinstein, a special thank you.

Marge Jacques, you were with me all the way through the birth of this book and you gave me courage when my own was failing.

Nina L. Diamond—Nina—we got it to flying! Your belief that I could do it and your encouragement was *beyond* helpful.

Thank you to Senator George McGovern and Dr. Brian Weiss. A special thank you to my friend and mentor, Dr. Elisabeth Kübler-Ross; my teacher, Susan Stavoy; my writing instructor, Bennie Blake; Nancy Leasure; and my agent, Linda Roghaar. Thank you also to my assistant, Cheyan Wolf. As I've often said, "Everyone should have a Cheyan in their lives."

And finally, a most grateful thank you to Ann LaFarge, my editor at Kensington Publishing, for championing my book, my ideas, my title, and for helping me to bring it all to a finish.

Introduction

We are at a pivotal point in the evolution of our planet and humankind.

Many of us already know—and, in the eternity of time, we are moments away from having proof—that there is life on other worlds.

We are about to go from our "one-world" idea of the Universe to join the "Bigger Universe"—the galaxies, where there is life everywhere.

To fulfill our destiny and to take our place among the galaxies, we must stop operating from our past patterns of *fear* and *war* and begin to come from a place of *love* and *peace*.

This change must begin in the hearts of each one of us. Each of us has the opportunity to assist in this process by *knowing who we are* and *being who we are!*

I believe that all of us have had many lives, that life is a continuum and that we've lived before on this world and others.

Whether you believe this or not, join me in my adventure of self-discovery. It is my journey from being a non-believer to becoming an intense believer/knower! It is my journey into finding the *meaning of life* on this planet and finding out *who I really am!* I've written it as an unfolding mystery so you can follow along and make the discoveries as I did.

It is also a journey with many dimensions and some of it will act as a trigger for your own self-discovery.

For those of you who'd like to work with your own discovery, I have included a short epilogue at the end of the book which outlines some simple methods you can use on your journey.

When I first started this book, I had no idea it was going to lead me to the conclusion that it did—that we all have karmic patterns and ultimately must learn to break them and end them.

All the things I've learned from the many years I've been an artist and been painting have transferred directly into writing. One of the biggest and humbling *knowings,* and one for which I'm most grateful, is that I do not do it alone. My guides and angels are with me each day when I'm writing, just as they are when I'm painting.

This is a true story. All events and recollections are recorded as I remember them, with the exception of some details that have been changed to protect people's identities. A few of the characters are composites of several people I've known and loved. Also, the names of lead characters as well as dates and places have been changed to protect people's privacy.

I've waited until the very last to write this introduction, for I've continued learning more about the path to the very end.

I'm grateful that it all happened and grateful to the people I've met through the happenings. They were all great teachers to me and the joy that I feel in life now is directly related to my learning all of those lessons.

Thanks again to all of you who have journeyed with me in this life and others.

While reading this book, you will meet Apollo, my four-pound psychic dog. Yes, he really does exist and he travels with me.

I hope somewhere on our respective paths we will meet and I know you will fall in love with Apollo.

PART I

All the World a Stage

Like the Gulf Stream invisibly pushing its
way to the Atlantic, our human mind
contains hidden currents urging our thoughts
and emotions towards a higher reality.
—DEEPAK CHOPRA
365 Days of Love and Healing

Chapter One

Changing Walls

Truth has no special time of its own
Its hour is now—always.

—ALBERT SCHWEITZER
Out of my Life And Thought

SPRING 1970 *A SMALL CITY ON THE CALIFORNIA COAST*

I heard the clatter of my heels as I bounced down the government building steps and welcomed the soft, comforting sound. It meant I was *here* and *now*, and not fading off from reality as I'd been doing lately.

But as I turned the corner the disorientation happened again. I blinked, struggling to retain any clear focus. I froze as a strange, damp mist began to form over my eyes. I shook my head, trying to drive away the thickening haze. It began to clear, but as my focus again became sharp, *everything* had changed! Heavy stone walls surrounded me, where moments before I'd seen modern, polished marble. A flickering torchlight played over the deep crevices of the large stone blocks that formed the walls and cast threatening shadows that reached like grasping fingers across the rough surface.

Dizziness. Confusion. I tried to walk on, but stopped again at the thudding sound of boots on the stone walk. Looking down, I saw heavy leather boots instead of the black pumps I'd so carefully polished that morning. My lavender silk blouse was now a tan leather tunic. Gone was all that was familiar—replaced by the now too-familiar feeling that I was losing my mind. Panic clutched at me, just as the fingers of the flickering torchlight clutched at the stone walls around me.

Dazed, I shook my head again, trying to drive away the fear as well as the immense panic and confusion. My mind was racing and so was my heart. I tried to calm myself by finding some cause, *any* cause, for what was happening to me.

I'm a philosopher—THINK, THINK—Is this really happening? Could it be possible that I'm seeing into another time? No, maybe I'm only dreaming.

I brought my fingers toward my face to pinch my flesh and see if I could bring myself awake. I felt a strong sting on my cheek as I saw my hand. *My God, my hand is that of a man.*

The place where I had pinched my cheek stung and told me I was awake. The flickering torchlight burned into my eyes like a blazoned prod that threatened my sight at the same time that it threatened my sanity.

I felt weak and frightened. I let my body fall heavily against the stone wall. Then I remembered a similar, desperate occasion when it had helped to close my eyes and block out all visual sensation. As I squeezed my lids tightly together, I could hear my heart pounding hard under the leather tunic. Digging my fingernails deep into the palms of my hands so I could still feel *me*, I waited, hoping that reality would return as it had on that other occasion.

After what felt like an unblessed eternity, I could no longer hear the thudding of my heart and I opened my eyes. The threatening torchlight was gone; it no longer burned into my eyes, only into my memory. The rough stone walls were also gone and the polished marble hall had returned. I let my hand run over my soft lavender blouse. The smooth, silken texture brought my fingertips alive. I lifted my foot, once again covered by a black pump, and bravely took a step, then another, and then another. As I walked warily down the marble hall, I listened to the comforting sound of my heels hitting the modern, polished marble.

Stopping in front of a door marked DRIVERS' LICENSES, I allowed my breathing to return to calm before I reached for the knob and pushed the door open. Inside I approached the small window labeled RENEWALS. Without looking up, a clerk handed me a form and muttered that I should step to a nearby table and fill out the form before returning to the window. I wished she had looked at me—it would have helped me to feel real.

I sat at the table, stared at the form, and then slowly filled in the spaces. My mind was still fogged and sluggish from what had happened only moments before.

To distract myself from the mantle of fear that hung over me, I let my mind flow into a patter of silliness. Why did people always object to telling their age? It never bothered me. In fact I looked forward to each new year and since antiques and things of the past gave me a creepy feeling, I always wanted to get away from the past as fast as I could. Then I once again felt the same icy fear grip me as I thought of the past and of time. I wasn't even sure I knew what time was anymore. I wasn't sure I knew what was in the past, or what was in the present, or the future.

I shook my head to clear it so I could go on, and turned back to the form that lay in front of me.

Occupation: ARTIST, I printed, slowly, deliberately.

Should I put "writer" down this time, too? I'd wanted to write since I was a child and had begun a female version of *Huckleberry Finn*. But I had never finished it and then had postponed writing for what I thought would be forever. No, I guess I would just leave it at "artist" for now.

I finished the form, stepped back to the window, and then went to the camera. I glanced in the mirror, grateful to see my familiar shoulder-length blond hair with usual windblown look. I brushed it with my hand. Combs never worked for my angora-fine hair. People were always making suggestions about what I should with it and I always wanted to tell them what they could do with their suggestions, but instead I would smile and say, "Have you ever tried to set an angora cat's fur?" They'd laugh, and so would I.

I removed my glasses. I didn't need them all the time, though I wore them more lately since my eyes had began to water in this misty fog. I turned to the camera. I saw my round, blue-eyed face reflecting back at me, thank goodness, and I smiled at my reflection.

Retracing my steps down the hall, hearing again the comforting sound of my black pumps on the polished marble, I dared to think back to what had happened only a short time before in this corridor: marble walls turning to rough stone, pumps turning to leather boots, and my hands turning from female to male. I wished it had been a dream; my still-throbbing eyes told me it had been more like a nightmare.

These disorienting, reality-shattering occurrences had been happening more and more frequently over the last few years. This one had been more vivid and had lasted longer than any of the previous ones.

What had happened to me back there? Was it possible that I was seeing into another time and that I was beginning to slip back and forth between then and now? What if I didn't come back the next time?

My senses exploded into an internal scream. I knew I couldn't handle all the sanity-threatening overload, and I shut down my mind. But I vowed that someday I would do *something* about these occurrences, that is, *when* I could. *If* I could.

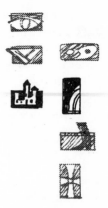

*C*hapter Two

Leilani

Each friend represents a world in us . . . and it is only by
this meeting that a new world is born.
                                        —ANÄIS NIN
                                        The Diary of Anaïs Nin

The red light on my answering machine was flashing when I got
home. I rewound the tape and listened. The call was from Honolulu.
"Hello, this is a message for Marilyn Sunderman," a voice said. "I
would like her to call me about doing a portrait."

I never knew where a portrait assignment would take me, not
only in the world, but in capturing someone's soul. I had learned
that by spending time with people—walking with them, talking with
them—I could get a sense of their outer being. Then I would go
deeply inside and allow my soul to tell me something about them
on a deeper level and how I should actually portray them.

I loved doing portraits. It gave me the kind of lifestyle I'd always
dreamed of. I got to do what I wanted to do, made a very good
living, and was able to travel all over the world doing portrait sittings
and art shows.

I also met all sorts of fascinating people and gathered many of
them as friends. I painted politicians, royalty, scientists, and actors

from everywhere. I'd always felt I'd one day paint a President of the United States, and though I'd painted President John F. Kennedy after his assassination and it ended up in Jacqueline's collection, it never really happened. I did a portrait of Senator George McGovern right after he'd lost his bid for the Presidency, and so at least I got as close to painting a living U.S. President as he got to being President.

It was on that trip to Honolulu that I met Leilani. Like me, Leilani was always looking for the meaning of life. We quickly became friends and would commiserate on life's purpose.

Leilani was one of those delightful, exotic mixtures the Hawaiian Islands are known for. She was part Hawaiian, Chinese, Tahitian, and English, all chop-sueyed together in a golden-toned skin that covered her delicate frame. Her eyes, like those of many Hawaiians, were huge and glowed like dark coals from under golden, long-lashed lids. Her hair, straight and black, hung nearly to her waist and swayed like palm leaves when Hawaii's gentle trade winds touched them. I'd never envied anyone's looks till I met Leilani.

For all of her exoticness, the most fascinating thing about her was her blend of beliefs. She was a devout Catholic, to the point that she actually took the Virgin Birth to be literal, yet she also believed in Oriental mysticism and practiced *Huna*, Hawaii's magical spiritualism.

As our friendship deepened, Leilani confided to me that she didn't know which belief to turn to for help with a particularly frightening phenomenon she was experiencing. When she first began to tell me about it, she glanced around as if to see if anyone was listening. I wondered if she was more afraid of what was happening to her, or that one of her priests—of the wrong belief—might overhear what she was about to tell me. When she turned back to me, her eyes glistened like dark pools as she whispered, "My house is haunted!"

Having revealed her secret, she brushed her blue-black hair off her shoulder and sat back in her chair, indicating she'd retreated into her protective shell and would say no more. But the bottomless black eyes continued to stare at me. She was wondering, as I was wondering, what to do next.

To fill the space, I began mumbling about not having any beliefs that could help her.

"In fact," I said, "I'm not sure I have *any* beliefs anymore. I think I gave them all up one day when I was a child, probably the same day I gave up a lot of my power." I found myself rambling into a story.

"When I was a kid, probably about five, I decided to join the rat race world." I watched Leilani's eyes to see if she was listening, to see if any sunlight reflected off the dark pools; then I continued. "Prior to that I was a real loner, always off in my own world, or some other world, creating something." Leilani vigorously moved her head up and down so that I knew she was not only listening to what I had said, but was also agreeing that I was probably from another world.

I laughed and went on, "So, I saw this machine in the field. It was huge. At one end of it was something that looked like a long tongue, and the men would throw the grain onto it. Then some of them would race down to the other end of it where stuff would fly out like it was defecating. I was absolutely fascinated by the machine and how it ran, so I decided to build one of my own—those chauvinists would never let me up on the machine. They said it was because I was too small—ha! I'm sure it was because I was a girl. My brothers weren't much bigger than I was and they were always on the machine."

Leilani started to laugh with me and I knew my story was serving its purpose, distracting her from some of her pain.

"Anyway, I decided that day I'd build a machine of my own. So I spent hours hammering and wiring pieces of wood together. I even found a chain to wrap around some small wheels so it could act like the tongue at the front of the machine."

Leilani was looking at me strangely and I laughed again, "Well, it looked like a tongue to *me* . . . and I thought it was alive, so . . ."

Leilani and I laughed even more as I went on.

"I really thought I had built some machine! As I remember it, it was incredible, with wheels up and down its sides, moving parts and everything. I thought all I had to do was sit back, tell it to run, and it would. Either I was terribly naive or I truly *was* from another world." I paused. Leilani was laughing and vigorously nodding her head up and down.

Thus encouraged, I went even further. "You see, I thought a person could do anything. All you had to do was believe you could. So when it didn't work," I shrugged, "at the ripe old age of five and a half, I just gave up all my beliefs."

Leilani continued to laugh as I went on. "But it was perfect, Leilani. After the machine, and with my being a Sagittarian, I've spent half my time being a party animal and the other as a philosopher looking for something to believe in."

The story had been a good diversion. Leilani looked at me, still laughing, and said, "Well, Marilyn, I have *too* many beliefs, so you can have some of mine."

The next thing I knew, Leilani was frantically shaking my arm. "Marilyn, Marilyn, are you all right?"

I looked at her for a moment, not sure who she was, as if I had just returned from another time or another world. Shaking my head, I tried to dispel the warm liquid that I had felt gathering around my eyes. I sat there dazed and frightened, not sure where I was or even *who* I was.

Wherever I'd been, for a few moments I had once again seen rough stone walls lined with flickering torches. It was clear to me that as these terrifying and disorienting experiences were coming more often, they were growing worse.

I could see that Leilani's fear for herself was now displaced by a fear for me.

That's when I decided to tell her about marble walls turning to rough stone, black pumps to leather boots, and about the flickering, grasping torchlight. But I also decided *not* to tell her how my hands had changed to a man's.

Chapter Three

My First Castle

There are small moments when I know ... those wonderful,
glorious, knowing moments ... before the doubt rushes in
and engulfs them in the darkening ...

SPRING 1959. A CASTLE IN EUROPE

I walked slowly down the rough stone corridor as I explored my
first European castle. Its blocks of limestone were huge and streaked
with marks from the many lives that had touched them. An old iron
bracket held an electrical fixture where once a torchlight had been.
The light from the fixture spread like a large, grasping hand across
the huge stone blocks and reached down into the deep crevices
between them, casting a steady, eerie shadow. By this faint light, I
could see the darkened, sooty patches made by the torches of another
time. Down the hall, just ahead of me, I could hear the sound of
student laughter and I followed it.

Just two weeks before, I had graduated, with honors, from the
University of Minnesota with a major in art and a minor in philosophy. During the summer of my junior year, I was given the exciting
opportunity to be a clerk at a large magazine in Chicago. I jumped
at the chance. Things got even better when the Art Director's assistant
quit, and I slid into the position. I knew it was a great opportunity
to learn some of the art business and I decided to stay on for the
entire year. By the end of the year I'd saved several thousand dollars.

It was a hard choice to leave my job, but I knew if I didn't, I might never go back to complete my art degree. As a philosophy student, I felt I was in charge of my own fate. As an impassioned, naive youth, I intensely desired to be a great artist. All of that, coupled with an unhappy love affair in Chicago, sent me dashing back to the University of Minnesota.

The Art Director had taught me to do pen line portraits for the magazine. Portraiture was something I hadn't studied at all in college, yet I took to it very quickly. One day he approached and said, "There's nothing more I can teach you about portraits. You already know more than I do. You must be a natural." I was thrilled that he thought I had the ability to do portraiture and I felt a whole new world was opening to me. When I returned to college, he arranged for me to continue to do portraits for the magazine. Thus, I was able to pay for my last year of college and have enough left over to go to Europe.

While I was growing up, there had never been a question in my mind about my going to college, just as there had never been a question about going to Europe.

I had been raised on a farm, an only daughter with three brothers. Being the only daughter, I was probably very loved, but I never felt like I was. My parents, trained in Minnesota stoicism, never really understood my dreamy nature and held me at a distance. Even more, I held *them* at a distance since I neither thought I knew them nor fit in. Farm life itself felt foreign to me and so did the people of this small midwestern farm community.

I preferred curling up in front of the TV and listening to a German or Italian opera on "Omnibus." I would also run across the fields blazoned with wildflowers and pretend I was in a meadow surrounding a castle and that the stream crossing the field was a moat. I'd splash through it, causing the tadpoles and frogs to scatter in all directions. I'd always known I would travel to Europe and explore castles and mountains.

The sound of student laughter was still ahead of me down the hall as I walked past a large, gilded frame hanging from the stone wall. Something about it caught my eye, so I glanced back and saw a portrait of a stiff, cold-looking young woman. A chill ran through my body when I saw her pale green eyes staring back at me. After a brief moment, I raced on to find my companions so we could head out for some drinking and partying in town.

That night we stayed in the castle, in rooms that had large feather comforters on the beds. As I sank down, down into the feathers, my thoughts returned to the portrait I'd seen hanging in the hall. I quietly slid out of bed, vowing someday to have a feather comforter of my own, and entered the corridor. I retraced my steps down the rough stone hall until I stood before the heavy, gilded frame.

As I stared at the woman in the painting, her pale green eyes again stared back at me. She was probably a Queen, I thought, as I noticed the crown on her soft, brown hair. I remembered having heard that the royalty of old did not bathe, applying perfume over the sweat of daily life. The young Queen's voluminous dress seemed to consume her as if no part of her flesh should show, or no scent should escape from her body. I imagined that she didn't shave her underarms or legs, either.

Her cold eyes stared at me from above a faded pink bodice that formed a triangle pointing downward from her throat. Her head sat smugly and stiffly upon the shelf of the velvet bodice. It felt as if, were one of the eyes to blink, her head would fall from its perch above the lace and pale pink, and I imagined it rolling across the floor and stopping at my feet. With the ridiculousness of that image, I felt as if I were experiencing something out of *Alice in Wonderland.*

Could she really have been that stiff and unfeeling, I wondered, or was the artist having fun and taking vengeance from his position of little power as an artisan in the Queen's court? Did he paint this portrait to take a swipe at the Queen who had the power to control his life or death? I wondered how much of this I was making up, and how much was because the artist had touched a deep, resonating core in me, now that I was also interested in doing portraits.

For a short moment a déjà vu feeling (had I been in this hall before?) flooded through me. I felt a slow, icy chill snake up my spine as the Queen's pale green eyes continued to stare at me, and I became immersed in an unusual, foreboding when I looked at the triangle formed by her bodice.

Enough of antiquity, I thought, trying to throw off the chill that still laced around me. I turned to go back down the hall to my room where I could bury my weary body amidst the soothing feathers of my bed.

The next day, I was compelled, almost obsessed, with exploring further into the castle. I walked past more rough-hewn stones that had been blackened by the soot of torches. The marks appeared like road maps to other times and lives and I could sense the presence of others who'd walked these halls.

An unexpected shudder flashed through my body as I walked

along the upper storey hall and passed the doorway that led outside and onto the roof of the turret that towered high above the deep green, densely wooded land below. As I stepped through the archway and to the turret, I gasped as if my breath had been pulled out from me. It was all I could do to look over the edge. I shook, not from the cold, but from—what? Heights had never bothered me before.

My eye caught the dark, murky water that filled the moat below and followed it to a small wooden bridge that was now permanently lowered for the hordes of tourists who passed over it every day. I looked up and said, "Thank you," to nothing or no one in particular. I wasn't even sure why I had said it, unless I was grateful that I didn't have to live in that day of moats and swords and queens who wore dusty, pale pink.

I stepped back from the turret just as a cold breeze grazed my cheek. The wind caught a strand of my hair and wrapped it over my eyes, leaving me sightless, as if a darkening was closing in over me.

I was not much of a believer in anything at that time, having given up formal religion as a young child, but for a brief moment I knew that there was more than just a breeze touching my face and more than just a blowing wisp of my own hair blinding me. Then for a second time I went into déjà vu and I felt I had been at that spot in the castle before, perhaps at some other time. A vision of the icy, pale green eyes that had stared at me from the portrait returned, but the thought was too frightening and too distant to be a memory, so I brushed at the hair clinging to my face and eyes. Then I turned to race back through the castle doorway, down the halls, and with a sense of needing to flee from the past, I bolted out into the daylight.

$\mathscr{C}$hapter Four

Sirens

A smattering of everything, and a knowledge of nothing.
—CHARLES DICKENS
Sketches by Boz

ONE WEEK LATER, GERMANY

"Trink, trink, bruderlein trink." The words rang out through the student beer hall. I tried to fake the German and laughed at how poorly I mashed the words and the accent. Jenny laughed along with me and we clicked our beer glasses in a toast. "To all the people who've ever walked castle halls, and to *fun!*" I quickly added.

Jenny was the perfect traveling companion. We were both fresh out of college, and both crazy about the craziness of life. We had met on the ship headed toward Europe. Heineken was only twelve cents a bottle and since we had survived the North Atlantic in a tossing ship with no stabilizers—and neither of us had broken any bones, as some students had—we thought it was a sign we were destined to explore and party our way together across the continent.

Jenny's narrow face was pixie-ish, as were her clear, pale brown eyes. Her soft, brown hair nestled neatly around her tiny face. On the many occasions when she laughed, a mischievous little rattle began deep in her throat and charged forth in a gigantic outburst.

"My college nickname was Sunshine ," I told Jenny. "Don't you think it suits me?"

"You are my Sunshine," she began to sing and then laughed boisterously at her own joke.

Jenny and I romped and played and flirted our way across Europe. On a moonlit night, we savored the warm, velvety waters of the Mediterranean for the first time, and on a bright, cloudless day we walked the cobblestone streets of the ancient walled city of Assisi. One evening over the Grand Canal in Venice, we danced with handsome Italians, a particularly memorable occasion, since the aged contessa who threw the party had leapt from her second-storey balcony into the canal with her dress flying high over her head, thus revealing that she was wearing no underpants.

Jenny and I felt that we'd broken the hearts of several young men as we stretched our wings over the continent. And we also climbed through castles together . . . *so* many castles.

Jenny and I had just come down the hillside from the Heidelberg castle. I was relieved that our tour of another part of the past was over. We lifted our steins, clicked them together, and then I said for no special reason I was conscious of, "To all those who have ever survived in dark castles."

Jenny looked at me strangely, and just then two young men approached us. Their English had a British overtone, like the English of most Europeans. They asked to join us and before we could reply, they pulled out chairs and sat down.

"I'm Gunther, and this is Claus," said the one with a deep scar. "We are students from here." As we laughed and drank together we searched for some subject in common that we could share.

They knew more of their country's history than I did, and it soon became apparent that it was important to them to express their sorrow over Germany's actions in World War II—almost as if they needed to apologize *to us* for it. Some of Gunther's swaggering confidence seemed to wane and his English became more scattered and broken as he said, "Humph—we—it's hard, our parents—they didn't tell us—maybe we—well, not again."

It was only about a dozen years after World War II, and some of the cities Jenny and I visited had sections where rubble still lay in courtyards, and where buildings were only bombed-out shells, reminders of the war. Each time I'd seen such ruins, it was as if I was trying to remember something horrible and I couldn't get away fast enough.

Claus had interrupted Gunther and tried to rescue him by offering his own apology.

Jenny and I only nodded. We were embarrassed at knowing so little about World War II, and our silence was accepted by them as absolution.

With *that* out of the way, their laughter and English returned and they drew our attention to the scars on their faces. The scars were pencil thin and sparely laced across their cheeks like small, red lines on a map. They were proud of the markings, and explained they'd received them from dueling with narrow, sharp-pointed swords. Both of them belonged to an elite student dueling fraternity—they stressed the "elite"—and they wore their scars like badges. I was not impressed, even though I'd already decided I'd rather be with the one with the deepest scars.

They invited us for a bicycle ride and a tour of the city. After a conference in the ladies' room, Jenny and I decided it would be another adventure and we agreed to the tour. I laughed as I jumped on the handlebars of Gunther's bike and almost split the tight skirt I was wearing.

We had gone only a few blocks when we heard the on-and-off pulsing of a siren. I immediately felt the hair rise in the back of my neck. I wasn't sure I'd ever heard such a wailing siren before, but somehow I knew it was the German *Polizei*. I tensed as a chill crept up my spine. We soon realized they were coming for *us*.

The boys began pedaling faster and faster, while Jenny and I began shrieking in panic. Our young duelists had lost all their English in their desperation to out-race the police. Jenny and I had no idea what was wrong or why we were being chased. The little I had read about the Gestapo was fueling the panic that now throbbed through my chest.

Just before we rounded a corner, I looked back to see Jenny and Claus fall from their bicycle and spill onto the side of the road, a very hard spill. Out of the corner of my eye, I saw that the deepest scar on Gunther's cheek had turned bright crimson. He had drawn his brow low over his eyes and was panting hard, obsessed by the need to escape the pulsing sirens. Driven by some inner chord or perhaps a secret fraternity code, he pedaled frantically, completely forgetting about Jenny and Claus.

Ahead of us a high wall stretched in both directions. Gunther jumped from the bike, pulling me with him. He didn't speak, he just mercilessly pulled me along. When we reached the wall, he half lifted, half shoved me to the top. As I tumbled over the wall, my skirt split nearly to my thigh. Gunther tumbled over the wall behind me. Then, spotting a large, brambly bush, he shoved me under it.

"What—what's, going on? Why are we running?" I gasped, as

soon as I could get enough breath. Gunther said nothing, just shoved his hand over my mouth.

Then I saw *them*. Standing just in front of the bush were the *high black boots*. I squinted out between the gnarled branches, hoping they concealed us enough to shield us from the boots. The storm trooper's legs were spread wide, and he held his hands tight on his hips. His high black boots reached all the way to his knees.

Then, as if remembering some horror from my past, I grasped the sides of my head between my clammy palms. They are Nazis, I thought. I began to rock back and forth as my panic rose.

"*Raus, raus*—out, out!" the storm trooper shouted.

"They're coming to get us, they're coming to get us!" I screamed in near hysteria, all the while rocking back and forth.

They pulled us from the bushes. My sobbing panic only grew as they loaded us into the back of a police van and slammed the heavy, steel-barred door.

At the station, my fear and sobbing was so intense that the police backed off. The pulsing siren, the black boots, and the chase through the German streets had unleashed a hysteria unlike any I'd ever felt in this lifetime.

"*Fraulein, fraulein, ist* okay," one of the black-booted men said to me.

I only sobbed and continued to shake.

Finally the *Polizei* ceased trying to calm me, and brought Jenny and Claus into the room. Seeing Jenny, seeing she was okay, brought great relief, and I stopped sobbing.

Then the uniforms came toward us again. "Away, away!" the *Polizei* ordered as they pushed Jenny and me to the side of the room.

In their desperation to have something to control, the police now turned toward Gunther and Claus. I could hear gruff orders, but could not understand their words. Finally I recognized the word "bicycle" and then something about two people riding one. Obviously there must have been a law against two on a bicycle and they also wanted to make an example of these two elite fraternity duelists who'd snared two unsuspecting tourists into breaking the law with them.

The *Polizei* now turned to Jenny and me and once again gruffly issued the orders, "*Raus, raus*," and I knew they were telling us to get out.

Jenny and I raced out the door. We didn't even look back at the two young men still being grilled at the table. Their apology for World War II seemed very far away and so did their good looks.

As we fled into the darkened German night, I knew I would not be able to explain the depth of my panic at seeing high black boots to myself or to Jenny. It was as if a window of time had opened and swallowed me back into Nazi Germany. And I was sure I never wanted to hear those wailing, on-and-off sirens again.

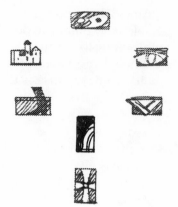

*C*hapter Five

Dark Chicago

All that we see or seem
Is but a dream within a dream.

—Edgar Allan Poe
A Dream Within a Dream

SEVERAL DAYS LATER, SWITZERLAND

Our student group had been invited to a special celebration. The menu was cheese fondue laced with lots of liquor, and the setting was a beautiful castle in the Swiss Alps. The tour leader circled the room, telling us that all of this had been mysteriously arranged by someone over the phone and through the mail, and that it was to be a special occasion for one of us. He continued circling, taking great delight in the fact that he was confusing all of us about where he would stop.

His delight over our continued confusion reminded me of a vulture hovering over an unsuspecting victim and I turned back to the fondue pot. Musical chairs had never been my game. I placed a piece of bread on a long skewer and dipped it deeply into the bubbling cheese. The guide stopped right in front of me and held out a small velvet box. I just stared until he thrust it at me and said, "Open it."

"What—what's this?" I stammered, as I opened the small blue box. I couldn't believe what I found inside—a large diamond in an antique filigree setting.

"Your engagement ring," he said, still gloating over the suspense he had been able to generate. "Madison J. Cooper has arranged this whole thing for you. This is your engagement party. Aren't you lucky!" The diamond was beautiful and a clear blue-white.

I wasn't sure I wanted to celebrate. It all seemed to be happening so rapidly and Madison hadn't even asked me to marry him, but soon I was caught up in the romance of it all and clicked each glass that approached me.

Meanwhile, Jenny just kept staring at me. I'd never even mentioned Madison to her. So later that night, I told her all about him, and about that last night I had spent in the United States, in Chicago, in his arms.

I had met Madison J. Cooper III the year I worked on the magazine in Chicago. He was the most exciting man I had ever met. Of course, growing up on a farm in Minnesota, that didn't have to be too far a stretch.

Madison was twelve years older than I, and I loved his air of sophistication. He had a tall, thin frame and long, slender fingers. Above his high cheekbones sat pale green eyes. He was not necessarily handsome, but he was brilliant and he was a writer, which fascinated me the most. He was working on the "great American novel," but earned a good living as a technical writer.

We had met at a bar called The Existential Mystic. All sorts of artists, writers, and would-be philosophers gathered there each evening after work. We thought of ourselves as the "Left Bank" mystics of Chicago.

I began discussing philosophy with Madison. His dark, unusual looks and his sophistication intrigued me, as did his confidence. He seemed afraid of nothing—except, perhaps, of not getting what he wanted.

After only a month, he asked me out. He drove up in a pale, dusty-pink convertible with its white top down. There was a box on the seat next to him. As I slid the box over to sit down, he informed me that we were going to Milwaukee for dinner and dancing. I frowned, knowing I was too casually dressed. He pointed to the box and said, "Open it." As I slid back the lid, a pale, dusty-pink, strapless gown emerged, exactly my size, exactly the color of the convertible. Maybe it was his worldliness, maybe it was that he had bought a gown to match the color of his car or that it fit me perfectly, but whatever it was, we went to Milwaukee.

Thereafter he loved to surprise me with gifts and the farm girl in me just kept growing more and more impressed. He was brilliant, and we spent hours discussing philosophy. Also, he always seemed to know how to dress and how to dress me.

We had dated for eight months when he invited me to meet his mother. It had been a passionate and unpredictable time. Though neither of us had talked about commitment, and in spite of the fact that he often became very jealous and acted as if he wanted to possess me, there had been hardly time for either of us to see anyone else.

We climbed the stairs to his mother's large, regal apartment. Once inside, I felt as if I were in an old European mansion. An elegant sophistication graced everything in the apartment and I knew it was this type of environment that had influenced Madison during his upbringing. His mother was seated in a stately, gold-gilded, Victorian chair. A little white poodle leaped from her lap and bounded toward me.

"Mother, I would like you to meet Miss Marilyn C. Sunderman," Madison said very formally.

As if ignoring Madison, she waved a hand that motioned me to sit in a high-backed chair across from her. The little white poodle jumped in my lap.

"Well, my dear," she said while pointing to the small animal that nestled in my lap, "this is Miss Magdalene. She has the run of the house and me, too, I fear." She spoke with a slight accent, which I couldn't place.

Madison went toward his mother and gave her a light peck on her cheek. I felt her almost wince from the touch of his lips.

Though it was clear that Madison doted on his mother, it was also apparent that she held a reserve toward him. He poured drinks for us and brought in delicately-cut hors d'oeuvres from the kitchen.

"My husband was a Prussian, you know. A General in the army." She put special emphasis on the word "general." "I'm afraid that being such a strict disciplinarian, he was very hard on Madison."

She paused and then drew her long, bony forefinger across her cheek so deeply that it left a red streak. "Then the war came—always men and their war games."

Out of the corner of my eye I saw Madison get up from his chair. She went on as if he wasn't in the room. "The General left for the war and never came back. Madison's older brother died in the Bataan death march, so there was only Madison left." She paused and shook her head slightly as if in disgust. "And he became a conscientious objector."

The small poodle on my lap began embarrassingly sniffing about me and started to do a backward and forward motion over my legs. I tried to push it away and I could feel my face turning red. Mrs. Cooper yelled at the poodle and clapped her hands together hard. It jumped from my lap and headed back to her, making the same motion upon her lap.

"I left Miss Magdalene with a woman friend when I went to Europe. When I returned she had this habit with women," Mrs. Cooper apologized, but seemed to make no further effort to stop it.

As Madison excused himself and went to the kitchen to make more hors d'oeuvres, she turned to me, her eyes darkening as they met mine. "How well do you know my son?" she asked. "Are you thinking of marrying him?"

Her questions caught me off guard and I stammered some kind of answer.

She pressed on. "I suggest you get to know him well, that you really think about it." Her eyes seemed to darken even more as she spoke. It appeared there was something more she wanted to say, the words held back behind her teeth and square, hard-set jaw. She stopped talking as Madison entered the room.

We never visited his mother again.

Madison received a work assignment in New York. It was a good one, he said, one he could not refuse. We parted, vowing our love, but made no commitment. I knew I still wanted to return to college. I also liked being single and knew I had the whole world to explore.

Shortly thereafter, I discovered I was pregnant. Though I had started dating another man, I was sure the baby was Madison's. I was devastated. What about all my plans for college, an art career, travel, and independence? Having a child would end it all. The laughter and play seemed to drain from me. I walked the cold streets of Chicago, sobbing. Should I tell Madison? Perhaps I should kill myself. Finally I called Madison and told him I was pregnant.

His first words were, "How do I know it's mine?"

When I heard that response, I felt that Madison had abandoned me and so I slipped even more deeply into despair.

I called the man I was dating, "I can't see you anymore," I said, my voice shaking as I started to hang up.

"Wait, wait," he shouted into the phone, "I want you to calm down and tell me what's up." He paused, "Now tell me why you can't see me anymore."

"Because I'm pregnant." I started to stammer something about him not being the father . . .

"Don't talk," he interrupted, "I don't care if it's mine or not." He was a well-known politician. I had met him through a friend, and soon we'd begun to date. I knew he had connections throughout the city and that he had a reputation he had to guard. "I'll arrange for an abortion," he said.

I hung up the phone, still shaking. I began more walking of the cold, dark streets of Chicago. With each block I felt the tall, grey buildings entrap me deeper in a prison of desperation.

Finally I called the politician. He arranged the abortion. It was a bad, botched, back-street abortion.

A week after I walked out of the doctor's office, I began to have severe cramps while several friends and I were out having dinner. I had to leave the table and I walked stiffly to the door, hoping my hand pressed tightly against my aching abdomen didn't give me away. Once in the alley behind the restaurant, I bent over, grasped my sides, and began to wretch. I prayed the snow catching in my hair would melt and take away some of the fire I felt in my body. One friend had followed me, and as she took my arm to steady me, she felt the blazing fever across my forehead.

"I'm getting you to a hospital," she announced.

"No, no, you can't," I gasped. "It would mean I would go to jail."

Abortion was still illegal at that time, so instead, she helped me down the narrow street that led to the doctor's office. We rang the bell for several minutes before the door opened and the doctor looked out.

"Oh, it's you, I knew you'd be back. Couldn't get it all before— you were too far along," he said, finally letting me in the door.

So without the aid of any anesthesia, in case the police came banging at the door, and for the second time, the doctor scraped my womb. This part of me that was already too painful to be touched was again cut and scraped and emptied.

The doctor told me the pregnancy was further along than he'd first thought and that he never should have performed the abortion at all. He wasn't sure what this newest complication would mean for the future, but that I'd better keep my mouth shut. I did not know at the time that I would never be able to bear a child.

Because my pregnancy had been so far along it was clear that the baby could only have been Madison's.

All the dazzling lights of the big city of Chicago had paled for me and there was just no play left in me. I decided to return to

Minnesota to finish my college degree—and never to speak to Madison again.

Back at the University of Minnesota, it wasn't the same. My enthusiasm for student life was gone and all that remained was the passion for learning and my desire to finish college as fast as I could. By doubling up on courses, I was able to graduate early. I prepared to leave for Europe.

Just before I left, a letter arrived for me. It was from Madison. He said he'd just returned to Chicago, had tried to find me, and that he still missed me. He made no mention of the pregnancy. I decided to stop in Chicago on my way to Europe. I was going to tell him off.

As I walked up the stairs to his apartment, I could hear soft, classical music coming through the open window. When he opened the door, I felt my heart race. He was tall and green-eyed and—more than I had remembered. I wanted to be angry and tell him how much I'd been hurt, but something happened to me. Maybe I'd become vulnerable because of the pain of everything that had happened in Chicago, maybe I still loved him, but I only stood there looking at him.

"Honey, I'm so sorry, I'm so sorry," he said, taking me in his arms.

The candlelight flickered. The champagne, the intimate dinner he'd prepared and served over European lace made me feel like I was in a dream.

Through the open window I heard the yowl of a cat. The howl pierced the quiet as Madison led me to the bedroom. It grew louder as the two cats began to make cat love and as the Tom thrust his body into hers, my moans began to keep cadence with the howls as Madison thrust his body into mine.

The next day I left for Europe.

Chapter Six

Dark Gathers

The lamb ... began to follow the wolf in sheep's clothing.
—AESOP
The Wolf in Sheep's Clothing

It was late in the evening when I finished telling Jenny my story. As I sank into the feathers of the Swiss comforter, darkness surrounded me and I drifted into dreams of places and things that had a familiarity about them. It was as if I was being prepared for the journey that would unfold before me and was being given all the signs: pale green eyes, faded pink triangles, black boots, castles with turrets, the struggle for power and control, and finally death.

I awoke with the phone ringing beside my bed.

"I will meet you in Paris." It was Madison's voice. "I've sold everything. I want to join you."

I glanced at the diamond on my hand. It sounded so romantic— a honeymoon in Paris.

"Yes, yes," I said, "I can't wait."

I hung up the phone, thinking of the signs that had just been revealed in my dreams, especially the struggle for power and control.

I flashed back to our visit with Madison's mother and to her admonition, "How well do you know my son?"

"Little," I mumbled to myself.

I arrived in Paris before Madison and instantly fell in love with it. So much of it felt familiar that I was sure it had been some cruel mistake that I'd been born on a Minnesota farm instead of on Paris's Left Bank.

The sounds and smells of the streets drew me into a romance with its past, as if it were my past, too. Sometimes I would have the déjà vu experience of knowing what would be around the next corner even as I was approaching it.

Soon Madison arrived, bearing gifts. He'd purchased a very complicated and expensive camera for himself and one only slightly less complex for me. On the first night he showered me with special "love" gifts. After that, nothing of my déjà vu experiences were the same. It was as if Madison's need to be the center of my attention took away my power of perceiving, not only of the past, but seeing the present with any clarity.

Before leaving the student tour I introduced Jenny to Madison.

"Oh, so you're *the* Madison that Sunshine has been telling me about," Jenny said with a laugh.

"I don't like the nickname Sunshine," was Madison's reply.

Madison and Jenny agreed to dislike one another immediately.

Jenny, when she could, took me aside and said, "He makes the hairs go up on the back of my neck."

Before she could finish what she was about to say, I laughed nervously and said, "He arranges my hair, too."

Jenny tried again. "He really gives me the creeps, Marilyn. I wish you'd get to know him better before you marry him."

After that, Jenny and I saw each other only a couple of times in Paris. I knew she wanted to say something more about Madison, but I didn't want to hear it. I was too adrift in my Parisian romance.

Madison and I spent our honeymoon on the Left Bank, *but without the benefit of a marriage license.* We roamed the streets and visited the sidewalk cafes. We could picture how the artists and writers of the twenties used to gather there. It seemed the perfect extension to our Chicago bar, "The Existential Mystic".

We rented a small flat three stories up and quickly learned the French way of always having apples by the bedside to freshen the breath in the morning. My first experience with a bidet was a disaster, since I didn't know what it was and as I bent over to examine it I got a face full of water. Madison found a small Russian cafe around the corner where everyone got to know us by our first names and teased us about being "the couple from Ou-S-Ah, who trying to get marry!" Madison didn't like the teasing.

We also found that it wasn't easy to get a marriage license in Europe. Somewhere deep inside me that was comforting, as if I wasn't sure about marrying Madison, but I also loved the romantic chase across the continent and the British Isles looking for a license.

We'd heard the tales of couples who for centuries had fled angered parents and been able to marry in Gretna Green, Scotland, so we raced north only to find we were a century too late to acquire a license there.

Sometimes I felt that Madison had us on a marathon to find a place where we could marry so that, with this license, I would become one of his possessions.

Finally, Madison said that we had exhausted all possibilities to get married, and suggested we go to Germany. He was sure that with his writing abilities he could find a job there.

Soon, Madison did find a job as a writer on the American Army base just outside of Nuremberg. He was told that when they could find him quarters he would have to live on the base. In the meantime, we snuggled into a small rented room and prepared for the approaching winter.

Many nights, after we'd made love, I would sink deeply into the feather comforter and in my dreams visit places that felt familiar. So often I would journey back in time to ancient castles, dark churches, and cobblestone streets. Then I would awaken and try to draw the memories' thin threads back to me before they could wisp away like spider webs blown apart by the wind.

Many times my dreams and nightmares seemed more real to me than my waking hours. I retreated into the world of my own thoughts whenever I could. When Madison was around, he wanted all my attention devoted to him and his needs.

Madison and I both loved to explore and one day he told me he'd planned a very special excursion.

We'd driven just a few miles outside of Munich when Madison stopped the car in front of two cement pillars. An iron arch, with a German inscription I could not understand, stretched high above the pillars. Between the pillars hung heavy metal gates with a chain laced through their middle bars.

A guard approached and Madison started talking in broken English, trying to tell the guard that he was a writer and wanted to do a story. He took out his passport and showed the word "writer" to the guard, while he pointed to the gate and made up and down scribbling motions across the writing tablet he'd pulled from his briefcase. The guard looked at me, and Madison pointed at the camera he'd given me, which was hanging around my neck. Finally the guard nodded, understanding that Madison was a writer and I, a photographer. He undid the lock attached to the huge chains and opened the gate.

We entered the World War II concentration camp of Dachau. Gaunt, pale people—the homeless left over from the war—were covered by soiled, torn clothing and stared out at us from an old wooden building off to the left. Through grey, tattered laundry hanging from a wire, I could see an open doorway and rows of bunks. Out of sunken, sallow faces, watery eyes peered out at me. A strange smell of something burned or scorched filled the air and everything else, too. As we walked, I rubbed my nose hard, hoping I could dislodge the charred odor and the vision of these homeless people.

We approached a ditch. I didn't know why it was there, but a strange feeling of familiarity came over me and I didn't want to look at it, or in it. I turned to a grey, pocked building in front of me and slowly entered its long hall. There were rows of hooks along the walls for clothing. I warily walked into the next room. It was made of solid concrete, huge and windowless. I looked up at the grey concrete ceiling and saw small pipes projecting downward. Talking to no one but myself, yet out loud, I started to say, "The show—ers," but the words caught in my throat.

I backed out of the room, out of the building, past the crematoriums with the charred smell still coming from them and continued backing, backing, stopping only when I stumbled at the front gate.

Madison and I drove back to the apartment in silence. I knew deep inside me there was knowledge about Nazi Germany. I didn't know where the knowledge came from nor was I ready to explore what it was that I knew. For me there were no words—only haunting, terrifying thoughts. I had mistaken the long hall with the hooks for a dressing room and had walked into the next room—the gas chamber—as innocently as I knew thousands of others had done only a few years before.

I ran the tub, entered it slowly, and lay there soaking for two hours. I could not go near the shower.

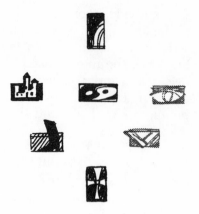

Interlude

It was raining outside. It rarely rained in Sedona. I got up from the computer and walked to the window. I watched a drop of rain fall from the roof onto the windowpane and slide slowly downward. I felt like that—like I was a small, small drop of nothing and was sliding slowly downward.

I felt that my writing was going poorly. Why was I putting myself through this? Why was I going back more than thirty years and dragging up old memories, some of them so painful that they had to be wrenched back, and then shaping them into a story? Why memories of my student days, traveling to castles, concentration camps, my marriage, another relationship, and then the panic and fear that was generated by the horrifying, reality-shattering occurrences when I would flash back to other times?

I was discouraged. Discouraged from getting up each day and writing—writing—and then going to bed and writing in my sleep. Why was I writing the story of my life, the story of all the pain and feelings? There must be a reason, something I'm to learn, a message in it all.

For over thirty years, I'd traveled to all corners of the world. I'd danced on the rooftop of an Istanbul hotel in the moonlight, watched a geisha serve tea in a pagoda in Tokyo, and stood in awe at the radiant, white marble of the Taj Mahal. And all the while I'd tried to dodge the thoughts of old, musty castles, high black Nazi boots, and pale green eyes that stared into my consciousness.

But also through all those years I was having more and more of those disorienting and reality-shattering flashbacks. They would always begin with a feeling of velvety liquid gathering around my eyes. I would be in a particular time and place, and the next moment, I would find myself in an altogether different time and place. The experience always left me dazed and terrified, but most frightening of all was that I could not find the reason or meaning for the occurrences, or a connective, comprehensible pattern. *Nor could I stop them.*

Then I'd found Sedona. Sedona is only two hours south of the Grand Canyon. It's mystical and beautiful. I'd tell people, "God designed the Grand Canyon, and she lives in Sedona."

Sedona became my cocoon, my safe haven, and I was letting all the collected feelings pour out as I searched for the connective link between the strange events and happenings in my life.

As I continued to watch the raindrop slide down the windowpane, I reflected back to when I first knew that someday I would return to writing. It was when the fear of losing my mind became so great, greater than the fear that circled me when polished marble walls turned to rough castle walls and black pumps to leather boots. Then I knew I had to write it all down in the desperate hope that I could find the commonality between all the events, the meaning of it all, or surely I would slowly be engulfed by the shadowy mire of madness.

But now as I stood watching the rain fall, staining the red rocks, I was not sure I could go on. I had spent my whole life trying to avoid my dark feeling. Now I was dragging up feelings that I had never handled and was not sure I wanted to handle. Touching areas I'd never faced, never thought I'd have to face, and I was weary.

I walked into my art studio and approached the mound of clay that was sitting on a high, rotating table. I pulled off the damp cloth that covered the shapeless form and stared at the deep red clay.

Mindlessly I began pulling small chunks of the clay from around the base of the mass and piled them higher and higher at the center. After the mound had become tall and thin, my fingers began forming a hood over the head I'd molded that was protruding from the top of the mound.

I looked down at the form that had taken shape. The shoulders were held in prayer. It was clearly a monk. I knew it was no accident that I had brought forth this reverent form. Perhaps I was looking at myself, one of my past lifetimes. This thought gave me a sense of calm.

Maybe, now that I saw myself like this, the flashbacks would not return again, or at least not so devastatingly. Maybe I could give up searching for answers, penning my memoirs, and just go on with my life. Maybe there was no need to probe deeper into places that were past and dark and painful. Maybe I should just be finished with writing.

So with the illusionary sense that there was nothing further that I needed to know than that I once could've had a life as a reverent monk, I put behind me the pallor and sadness of the visit to the concentration camp. I walked into the bedroom and lay down on the cool whiteness of the feather comforter I'd finally bought myself. Apollo, my four-pound papillon dog, followed me. We often meditated together.

As I lay there, the feathers seemed to swallow me, pushing up around my body as I fell into a deep sleep.

I awakened holding my left leg very stiffly, as if it were frozen. It felt weak and fragile, as if it would pull apart if I moved it. I knew it was infected and that the infection might be life-threatening. It took me a while to realize that my leg was actually still intact and that I had only been dreaming.

I knew the dream held some keys to the events I'd been writing about and for days after that I promised myself that I'd write it down, but I found that I didn't even want to think about it. Most dreams are vague and wispy like spider webs, but this one was always there in front of me, too disgusting and nauseating to face.

Finally, on the fourth day, I grabbed a small pad and wrote down all I could remember about the dream *and the eye* that had stared back at me from my lower left leg.

THE DREAM

My lower left leg was covered with dried, flaking seed pods. They were lined up side by side and were forming the shape of a strange, mystical eye. When I stood, it was as if the eye was on end and looking at the world askew, but when I lay down the perfect shape of an eye stared back at me.

I felt the pod's dry husks no longer held any live seeds and this indicated the area had been healed for a long time. I would only have

*to brush them away to allow the deep pink flesh underneath to finally
be exposed.*

*I scraped the disgusting husks away and discovered there was live
infestation underneath. I began to dig deeper and deeper into the
center of my leg, searching for the still-festering seeds that were eating
away at my flesh and my foundation. I finally, as if by accident, pulled
a large segment of bone from my leg. In deep terror, I now realized
that all that was holding my leg together was the surface skin and
that my left leg might have to be amputated.*

The dream was immensely repulsive to me. I had to calm myself
just to look at its meaning.

I drew a line down the center of a page in my note pad. On the
left I put down the key words from my notes, words like: mystical
eye, seed pods, festering, foundation, left leg. Then on the right side,
after each word, I put what it meant to me. I really didn't know
what the "mystical eye" was about, but it was clear that "festering"
was like an infection and "foundation" was about my strength, my
own foundation.

The whole dream still upset and nauseated me immensely and
though I tried hard to find its meaning, even with all my techniques
for interpreting dreams, none seemed to get to the essence of why
the dream was tearing at me so much.

More days passed. While I was walking Apollo by a slightly
wooded area in Sedona, I looked over and saw a rabbit sitting no
more than three feet in front of us. I was amazed that she wasn't
afraid of me. Apollo had not yet seen her. I stood staring at the rabbit
for minutes as she stared back at me. Was she hypnotized or was I?
She sat perfectly still, as if she thought that in this frozen state she
could go unnoticed forever. Then in an instant she unfroze, leaped
up, and bounded away.

That's when Apollo saw her, and that's when, as if in a flash of
insight, I understood the meaning of the dream: I could sit frozen
just as the rabbit had, frozen in my feelings, hoping my painful state
would go unnoticed—frozen like my left leg in the dream—or I
could bound into life. Like the rabbit's eye staring at me, the dry
husks of old events were staring at me. Under it all was a deep
wound and live seeds of hurt still festering in my left leg—my LEFT
LEG—LEFT—WHAT WAS LEFT? What was left was the unhandled
pain and hurt, and finding the final connective links between my
past patterns of destructiveness.

That's when I knew why I was writing again: by tracing the

patterns and their connections I would find the meaning of it all and release it, so that, like the rabbit, I could claim my freedom and bound into the rest of my life. I looked at Apollo—sweet, sensitive, intuitive Apollo—and he was looking back at me, his head cocked as if he, too, was searching for meaning.

"Let's get on with our lives, you little stalker." I'd recently begun affectionately to call him that since he always followed me everywhere.

We walked back to the computer room and I started taking myself back in time to my marriage in Germany.

Chapter Seven

The Marriage

Be willing to accept the shadows that walk across the sun ...
—EMMANUEL
Emmanuel's Book II, The Choice for Love

Madison was proud of the small German car he had bought and gunned the motor as we forged up the steep hill leading to the castle. We heard laughter and noticed two people struggling on a small path next to the road. The area was thick with trees. Madison stopped the car and yelled to the couple.

"Hello, would you like a ride?"

Noticing us for the first time, they stopped walking and approached the car.

"Hallo, we—ya—like a ride," the man replied in broken English.

The couple climbed in; the man had to stoop considerably to fold his large frame into the back of the small car.

"I bist Hans, this my Frau Gisela," the tall, handsome, square-jawed man said.

Hans was much older than Gisela. Gisela had blond hair, blue eyes, and could have been my older sister. "We live in villach near—Ansbach," he said with a big smile to show us that he appreciated not having to climb further up the steep hill to the castle.

Gisela spoke no English, Hans a little. Gisela and I instantly liked each other and tried to communicate with broken words and lots of hand gestures.

The four of us spent the day together, and as we drove we turned each time Hans told us to. Finally, Hans and Gisela took us to a local Hofbrau House and amidst the um-pah-pahs of the music, introduced us to the German equivalent of a hamburger. A patty of raw meat sat in the center of a plate surrounded by onions, capers, anchovies, and two raw eggs. Staring at the two eggs, with them staring back at me, I felt as if I might have another disaster like I'd had when I'd first come eye to eye with a bidet, but Gisela showed me how to mix it all together and hoist it onto a thick-crusted slab of bread. And to my amazement, I found I liked it.

Sometime during the day, Madison had told Hans about our plan to get a marriage license. Hans vowed to help him find a way.

The four of us met often. I kept trying to learn some German, Gisela English. We made a pact to swap languages. Hans acted as the interpreter when we got stuck on a word or thought.

Hans and Gisela were always free when we called, as if they had no other friends. This seemed curious to me, but I grew to accept that just as I did Hans's strange moods.

Little by little, we learned more about them. They were married, but Hans always held Gisela at a distance. They never discussed having children. Hans was already a young man when he was drawn into World War II. He swiftly rose in rank and was proud that he'd learned to fly, though he clearly stated he never wanted to again. He had an ex-wife somewhere, but he didn't know where she or his grown children were. "It was the war," he said. "It drove everyone apart." Then he went into one of his moods, looked away, and turned silent.

Gisela didn't talk while Hans was talking. She would wait until we were alone and then share with me in the little English she was quickly learning. Often I felt that Hans abused her. I was afraid of him just as Gisela had told me she was afraid of Madison.

When word came that quarters were ready for Madison at the base, we were told that I wouldn't be allowed to live with him until we had a marriage certificate. I considered it great sport to sneak through the window and into his quarters until the night I was caught half-in, half-out of the window in my nearly nothings.

The next morning the very formal base commander called me to his office. He thought of himself as fatherly. "Miss Sunderman, we can not have you sneaking into the compound as you've been seen doing." As if reading my thoughts, he continued, "Yes, I know you think of yourself as married, but until you can show me a marriage certificate, German or American, we do not consider that you are."

I was embarrassed as well as furious. I certainly *did* feel married and I was totally torn with indecision. Returning to the United States was out of the question; since I had no money left, I didn't want to stay alone in Germany, and Madison *had* to stay on the base. Finally, Hans and Gisela invited me to stay with them, where Madison could come and visit me. They had a small yet comfortable two-bedroom apartment in a nearby village.

I'm not sure when or how it was that I found out that Hans had been an S.S. Captain. Maybe he had told me before I realized the extent of its meaning, maybe it was the old yellowing photo that hung by the living room door. It showed Hans, young and handsome, in a black Nazi uniform. He stood proudly in a group of men all wearing the same uniform and with the same high black boots. One of them held a flag with the swastika clearly showing. I shuddered when I saw the high black boots, but even more at the sight of the swastika.

I'd been at Hans and Gisela's for two months; I liked sharing with Gisela and we'd become very close. Being able to help around their apartment made me feel useful and made up for not spending any time painting or drawing.

They had no refrigerator, so each day I would go to town to do the marketing from the list Gisela would give me. As I walked down the narrow streets, my heels would make a tapping cadence on the cobblestones that felt strangely familiar. I couldn't shake the feeling that I'd walked before on these streets or similar ones, and strangely, speaking German seemed to come very quickly and easily for me.

One day, around noon, the apartment door opened. This was unusual, as both Hans and Gisela worked late. Hans walked in, a strange smile on his face, his dark grey eyes slightly glazed. He'd been drinking. He sat down on the couch and motioned for me to sit beside him. I shook my head.

"Sit down here!" he said gruffly, as if in command.

I shrank back from him and said timidly, "No."

He rose, staggered toward me, and stood there towering over me, his beer breath blowing across my cheek. I began to move away, but he grabbed my arm and tried to pull me to him. My blouse ripped when he yanked at my buttons. I threw up my hands, forcing a space between my chest and his.

"Hans—Hans!" I screamed, "Think of Gisela!"

Suddenly, his eyes went distant. He let go of my arm and my blouse, turned, and then stomped out of the apartment.

After that incident, I was always on edge at the apartment, jumping whenever I thought I heard the door. I couldn't tell Madison. I was afraid of what would happen between him and Hans. They were both so proud, and so aware of what belonged to them, like "their women".

One day I overheard Hans's voice in the other room. He was pacing and shouting. "Why don't they leave us alone? It's been long enough." Through the partially opened door I could understand enough German to know that Hans was angry and worried. The authorities were looking for ex-Nazis, arresting them and trying them for war crimes.

"It will only be a matter of time before they find me," he roared. He talked about forging documents and fleeing to South America.

I never let Gisela or Hans know that I had overheard them. We ate in silence, chewing the raw smoked bacon I'd learned to eat without gagging. I would cut a thicker-than-normal slice of hard-crusted bread and lay the bacon across it before eating it. Gisela and Hans never knew I didn't like it. I had ceased trying to tell them that in the United States we fried it before we ate it. And I didn't know how to say "no, thank you" without appearing to be rejecting their hospitality. I also was becoming more afraid of provoking *any* reaction from Hans.

One day Madison burst through the door in great excitement. "We have the marriage license, but we have only two hours before the office closes for the weekend." He grabbed my hand and pulled me toward the door. He also had Hans in tow, and told him he should drive to get Gisela and meet us in the office at Ketterbach, the county seat.

It did no good to tell Madison I needed to change clothes before I got married. So that's how I ended up in a black skirt, a black tight-fitting sweater with a black hood covering my head on my wedding day. There was a little of the eccentric philosopher inside me that knew it would make a dramatic story back home in my folks' small farm community if I said I was married in black. I had little idea at the time how appropriate being shrouded in black would actually be.

Madison's map led us down the road to the smaller-than-small village of Ketterbach. There were no more than thirty houses in the town, maybe less. It seemed that the only life on the streets was a sooty man in a dark suit carrying a long pole over his shoulder. He wore a tall, formal top hat. It was creased halfway up its crown and pitched forward at a perilous angle that was the exact opposite of his soot-covered nose. It looked like something out of *Mary Poppins* and I laughed and pointed, saying, "Look, Madison, a real live chimney sweep." Madison laughed along with me, then furrowed his brow and raced on.

We found the building with the official marking. Hans and Gisela were already waiting there.

The offices were dusty, old, and dark, but the shades were drawn so you couldn't tell exactly how dusty. Madison presented the certificate and the clerk shook his head. He stood for a long time looking at us as if his stare could make us go away or at least stall us until he could figure out what to do with us. Finally, he motioned to the door and said something we could not understand. Hans pushed us back out through the front door as he told us that the clerk wanted us to go have our wedding feast and return in an hour. Then he would be ready for us.

I didn't feel like a wedding feast and I was growing more and more uncomfortable about being dressed in black. It certainly didn't fit the dream I'd always had of my wedding outfit and maybe it wouldn't be such a great joke back home after all.

But Madison wanted the wedding *now*. We went around the corner to a local Hofbrau House and he ordered us all some schnapps. I started to protest, but he just shoved it in front of me said, "Marilyn, drink this." Then, seeing my look of dismay, he put his arms around me and withdrew a box from his jacket.

"Here, honey, I've been saving these for this occasion. Open it now, 'Mrs. Madison J. Cooper III-to-be."

Inside the box was a beautiful, eighteen-inch strand of shiny, gorgeous, unmatched black pearls. How fitting that they were also black.

"Thank you, Madison, I love them." I drank the schnapps.

One hour and many drinks later, we entered the small office again. The clerk, who Hans informed us was the Mayor, had done his best to transform the dusty, dark office into a wedding chapel. He had draped white sheets everywhere, over countertops, desks, and chairs. The room looked more like a summer place being closed for the season than a wedding chapel. Two scraggly plants, almost devoid of leaves, had been placed atop one of the counters. Maybe because of the schnapps, maybe because of the ridiculousness of it all, I laughed, threw up my arms, and saluted, "On with the show!" So, with a ceremony in a language I could not understand, dressed in black and standing in a small, sheet-draped office in a tiny village in Germany, I became Mrs. Madison J. Cooper III.

The schnapps also wiped out any thoughts of the warnings that had come from Jenny, Gisela, and Madison's mother.

Both Madison and I were glad we'd already had our honeymoon in Paris—we were exhausted. Later as I lay in his arms, I could hear him softly say over and over, "You are mine. You are mine."

The very next morning, Madison paraded into the Base Commander's office—with me in tow. His eyes narrowed as he laid the signed marriage certificate on the commander's desk. I knew there was a power struggle going on between these two men and I knew that Madison now had the papers to emerge the winner.

That day I moved into the small German community that served the base near Nuremberg.

Only one week after our wedding, Madison started to exert his power over what he thought of as his latest possession—me. We had been out keggling (a German form of bowling), and then drinking. I had worn my wedding outfit, the short, black skirt, the tight-fitting black sweater with the hood, and my black pearls. Madison liked me in it, said it made me look very sexy, and insisted that I wear it.

When we returned to the quarters, Madison was loud, drunk, and hostile. He accused me of flirting with one of the German men who'd been at the next lane and also lived in the compound community. Nothing I could say would calm him. Yes, the man had stared at me often, but knowing Madison's jealousy, I had always looked away and kept my distance.

Madison had given many signs that he was jealous and possessive, but never like this. Now I knew why I had been so fearful of this part of him. His drunken ravings about the German man grew more and more hostile.

"I saw him undressing you with his eyes!" He started toward me. "You're mine and I want what belongs to me—NOW!"

He tore at my clothes. The stale smell of liquor and his ranting turned me cold and I pushed him away. His shouts grew louder as he grabbed at me again, this time making a large tear in my sweater and sending the black pearls scattering in all directions across the floor like so many frightened beetles. His pale green eyes darkened and that terrified me. I struggled to break free and run from his rising anger.

Suddenly, I felt his fist crash into my face. My teeth ground against each other as his other fist struck my jaw. I tasted blood in my mouth and it filled me with even more fear. I lifted my hands toward my face to try to protect myself from the barrage of his fists as he continued to pound into me. I felt a sharp, piercing pain at the bridge of my nose, then heard a crack as one of his blows landed across my cheekbone. Then another blow caught the side of my head, and after that I could only hear a ringing hum from my throbbing ear.

Again I tried to raise my hands to protect myself, but he lashed out, grabbing my hair. I felt huge clumps of it being pulled from my head as he pushed me backward onto the bed. He pounded his fists again and again at my face and then all over my body. The last thing I remember before blacking out was the suffocating feel of his hands closing tightly around my neck.

I don't know how long I lay there, blacked out. When I awoke, I was naked, bloody, and bruised. I felt heavy and drugged and my face throbbed. Madison was stretched out on his back, passed out, his feet dangling over the side of the bed.

I grabbed my coat, threw it over my naked, aching body, and raced barefoot down the steps and out into the snow. I ran screaming through the streets of the village yelling, "HELP, HELP!" A few shades lifted as I passed by. Eyes peered out at me, but no one, *no one* unlocked a door. In desperation, I'd forgotten all my German, or even that I was in Germany, and I was futilely yelling for help in English.

A couple of blocks later a door opened. A young girl, perhaps eighteen or younger, stood in the doorway, arguing with the man behind her. She wanted to let me in. When he saw that it was me he stepped to the door, threw it open wider, and said, "In, in."

It was the German man Madison thought I was flirting with. He continued to eye me as his girlfriend brought towels and warm water to bathe the blood from my face. Finally I was calm and he motioned her to step aside. He took my hand and led me to the bedroom.

"I want you to get some rest, some sleep. You can have the bedroom," he said. I looked back to see his girlfriend shaking her head and lifting her hands in a motion that suggested helplessness.

I was so weary I could only follow him. He laid me down on the large comforter and twisted my bruised body to remove my coat. I felt him slip into the bed next to me. I was too weak and beaten to fight anything, any man. I could only groan as his hands flowed over my sore body and his teeth bit into my breast. I knew I was being raped and I could not stop it.

The next morning I was pushed out the front door. Still barefoot, still with only a coat to cover my naked body, I retraced my steps back through the snow. I was afraid, confused, and knew that Madison would try to kill me again, especially since now he'd be right about my infidelity with the German man.

I knew that there was no police station in this community, and I thought I would be raped again if I were to turn to another rescuer.

I stood a long time in front of our quarters. My feet and my hands were freezing. My mind then froze on a picture of my battered body after I'd been found murdered in a little village in Germany. Finally, when I could no longer stand the cold, I climbed the steps to my waiting death.

Slowly, slowly, with each step, I felt I was tracing a dance between life and death. The cadence of one step: "You will live." And with the next step: "You will die."

I stood at the door. I heard no sounds. I grasped the knob and turned it slowly as I pushed open the door. Glancing about, my heart racing, my eye caught sight of a bruised, swollen face. I gasped when I realized it was my face reflecting back at me from a mirror. I would not have recognized myself.

Madison was not there, so I approached the mirror cautiously. My right eye was black and nearly swollen shut. My forehead, on the right side, jutted out inches, nearly covering my ear. My nose was not there—it was lost under the swelling crossing the center of my face. My jaw was swollen grotesquely to the left. My whole face looked like a pumpkin squashed crosswise. I lowered my head so I could see in the mirror the huge area on my head where my hair had been ripped out. My face hurt too much for me to cry so I only let small tears roll over the lids and down the swollen mounds that had once been my cheeks. The tears hit my mouth and I tasted salt.

Madison approached from behind—I hadn't heard him over the sound of my own pulse pounding in my shattered eardrums. When his hand touched my shoulder, I jumped and screamed.

In an instant he was in front of me. I was terrified as he grabbed my arm. I tried to pull free so I could run, but he continued to grasp my arm in his vise-like grip as he studied my face. Still holding my arm, he fell to one knee and began to rock back and forth as he said over and over, "Honey, I'm sorry, I'm so sorry."

When I realized he was not going to kill me, I slumped into a chair. Madison paced and pleaded, paced and pleaded in front of me. Then he began scurrying around retrieving the fallen, scattered black pearls, as if piecing them together could piece together our shattered marriage.

"I'm so sorry, I'm so sorry," he kept repeating. Finally he said the only thing that I really heard: "Honey, let me take you home."

Madison arranged for two tickets to sail out of Rotterdam. He said it was all he could afford with the little money we had left. I suspected he only wanted to keep me in Germany longer so I could not flee from him or so that there would be more time for my wounds to heal before we arrived back in the United States, or both.

The only thing I wanted to do before we left was to say goodbye to Gisela. Less than a week had gone by, so I was still very swollen. My right eye was nearly swollen shut and the purples were deeper. My face was still the most bruised and battered sight I'd ever seen in my life.

Gisela opened the door. Madison began giving the explanation we had discussed—I had been in an auto accident. Gisela flew at him in a fury, her fists pounding over and over at his chest as she yelled, alternating between English and German and in her heavy accent, "You did thes to her—Ou did thes to her!"

Hans was standing behind her and when he had taken in the full scope of the scene and my face, he began a deep, almost fiendish, laugh that continued on and on until he was doubled over. I was hurt and bewildered—why was he laughing? Gisela finally took me in her arms, led me to the side of the room, and we both wept as she rocked me like the small battered and wounded child that I was.

Chapter Eight

New York

WINTER 1959

It was cold when we left Rotterdam. It was cold when we arrived in New York. We had only $6.00. Before we left Germany, I sneaked away and placed a collect call to New York to two college friends who now lived there. I was still afraid of Madison, but I didn't tell them that. What I did tell them was another lie: I had been in a serious auto accident and we were returning to the United States on a Holland American ship called the *Rotterdam.* I had not told them the date; I'm not sure I even knew it.

"Sunshine, Sunshine!" I heard the voices yelling over the sound of the ship.

Julie and Scott were standing on the dock, waving and shouting as the ship came in. I was so happy to see them I wanted to jump over the side and race into their arms for protection. Instead, my fear of Madison gripped me and I clung white-knuckled to the railing as the tears spilled from my eyes and down over my still-swollen cheeks. It seemed so long since I'd been called Sunshine, since I had *been* Sunshine.

While aboard the ship, I became more frightened of Madison and went to the ship's doctor. I told him my husband had beaten me and asked him if he could help me after we arrived in New York.

He told me he could not. He then examined my face and informed me that I had a fractured skull, a dislocated jaw, and a broken nose. He said the only thing he could do was give me a brace for my nose so it wouldn't bend so much. He wanted to ask Madison for the money for the brace, but I told him if he went to Madison it would surely be my death warrant and pleaded with him not to. I wasn't sure whether he would or not and became even more frightened, especially since I was now convinced no one was willing to help. Madison had become suspicious after he'd seen the brace, but believed me when I told him the doctor thought I'd been in an auto accident.

After disembarking, Julie looked at me and then at Madison, shook her head, and then folded her arms around me. I began to cry as she whispered in my ear, "Auto accident, my foot." Julie had always been intuitive and I knew she could see through the lie. Julie also made it clear to Madison that she would continue to call me Sunshine.

Julie and Scott had a small, humble flat in the Bronx, but when they opened their doors to me, it felt like I was being invited into a mansion, and I felt *safe* for the first time in a long while. I wanted to open up, to tell them everything, but Madison was always there watching me, staring at me with his pale green eyes, so I didn't talk about him or Europe. Also, I couldn't remember anything good about Europe or my marriage; it was as if it had been beaten from me. Madison was in a hurry to find a job and a "place of our own to start over." He assured me that everything would be different now that we were "home," that whatever happened in Europe had only been "Germany and foreign things and foreign people." I was not so sure.

Within four days he had a job and within two weeks he came back with the news that he'd found an apartment on the lower west side of Manhattan.

I didn't want to leave Julie and Scott's. They made me feel safe and wanted. We had known each other from the first college I'd attended. Julie was warmer and brighter than she knew. She could nurture anything in anyone and help it grow—she was doing that for Scott. She worked as a credit manager for a large department store while he finished his master's degree in business.

Julie tried to nurture me so I could regain my confidence. More than the beating to my face, I had received a beating to my ability to trust myself and the world. What had I done to cause Madison to try to kill me? Gone were my ideas of my independence, of an art career—they had been shattered along with my cheekbone that cold day in Germany. Madison talked faster than my dimmed, broken mind could follow so I felt I had to believe him when he told me it would never happen again.

With great reluctance, I moved out of Julie's and followed Madison into the dark bowels of Lower Manhattan. Within a week the beatings resumed. He would become jealous, he would become upset, then he would be sorry—always afterward he was sorry. I dipped more deeply into a dim, shadow world. Should I never disagree with him? Should I never speak at all? Was this what I deserved?

Scott flopped the newspaper down in front of me. A headline read, WIFE KILLED BY HUSBAND. "I don't want to read about *you*," he said. Julie and Scott had called me and said they urgently needed to meet with me—alone. I had arrived thinking it must be something important. I looked at the paper, then rejecting their concern and my own feelings, I slipped deeper into a position of denial as I pushed the paper away and resumed sipping my coffee.

By this time I had lost any belief that I was in charge of my own fate and thought that it was more likely my fate to one day be killed by Madison. I told myself it was my fault, that I could never find the right words when I was around him, and that's why he became so angry. I would just have to try harder.

I had gotten a small job selling children's wear at Saks Fifth Avenue and always came home immediately after work. I never went out and Madison didn't want me to see Julie and Scott anymore so I'd sneaked out to meet them that day when Scott showed me the newspaper headline.

Days later Madison returned from a short business trip. He was hot and tired and had had several martinis on the flight back. Earlier, I'd dashed out, gotten two steaks (rare for our budget), and a nice bottle of wine. "What have you spent our money on? Where did you get the money?" he demanded. "Who were you with?"

This time I got furious with him and his jealous behavior. The last time I had seen Julie, she had wrapped her arms around me and said, "Sunshine, I love you. Remember, you are wonderful," and for a brief moment I had seen a small light reflect back at me from her eyes. Her nurturing had awakened some feeling in me that perhaps I would be all right, perhaps I could be Sunshine again and perhaps I deserved more.

I felt I would wait for the right moment and then begin a discussion with Madison about our future. I knew when he'd been drinking was not a good moment, so I walked away from him as he ranted. I went to the shower to cool off and to let him cool off.

As I stood under the cool water I heard the shower curtain draw back. Madison's narrowed eyes raged. He had lifted the glass percolator from where I'd brewed coffee for our special dinner, and now stood in front of me, weaving. Then, with a quick single motion, he threw the boiling coffee all over me. The glass pot slipped from his hand and hit the front of the tub. Scalding coffee and shattered glass flew all over my naked body, and I screamed out in pain. I was afraid to move my feet; there was glass everywhere. I reached to the tap and turned the water higher. Cool water poured over me and sent the hot coffee flowing down the drain. Small red beads of blood formed and covered my stomach and legs from the tiny splinters of imbedded glass. My resolution and strength had been shattered along with the coffee pot.

Madison saw the blood that was forming on my body and reached toward me. I shrank away from him and cowered in the corner of the shower. I feared his blows and I felt they would be the next thing to shower down on me. He grabbed me. As he held my body he began to brush the specks of glass from me and the blood from the cuts to his hands now mingled with my blood.

I screamed and tried to push him away.

"Honey, I'm sorry, I'm so sorry." He started racing around, picking up the shards of glass. He continued, "I'm sorry, so sorry," as he got slippers to cover my feet. I was still afraid of him, but I let him touch me as we spent hours picking the small pieces of glass from my body. I really couldn't talk. He finally stopped talking. After the fear and shock I only felt numb, and I vowed never to let this happen again.

I began to make plans to get away. I needed money. I needed a place to go. I knew I had to think of a way to tell Madison after I'd moved out, but without telling him to his face; I was afraid of what he might do if he lost his possession—me—and anyway, he could always out-talk me. I found a small room just blocks from where we lived. It was so small that it only had room for a single bed, and there was no closet. I thought, what do I need with a closet, I don't have any clothes anyway.

I wrote a carefully worded note telling Madison I had left him: I would never see him again unless it was in a psychiatrist's office; I would call him at a certain hour at his office—I felt I owed him that. I folded the note, put it in an envelope, and took it to where he worked when I knew he would be at lunch. I handed it to his boss, told him briefly that I was leaving Madison, and asked that he give him the note and be there for Madison when he read it. He said he was sorry to hear I was leaving and assured me that he would personally give Madison the note and wait while he read it. I left walking taller than I had in months.

I was sitting with Julie at the appointed hour. I touched her hand for reassurance as I got up from the table, went to the telephone, and called Madison. His voice was calm, gentle, pleading. He had arranged an appointment with a psychiatrist for that night. The fact that he could arrange it so quickly took me by surprise and knocked me off my guard.

"Please, please, meet me there," he pleaded. "We will work it all out."

Somewhat dazed and forgetting Julie's cautioning, I promised to meet with him at the psychiatrist's office.

Hairs rose on the back of my neck as I walked the street on the northwest side of Manhattan that lead to the psychiatrist's office. It was approaching dark and the light from the street lamps cast grasping, eerie shadows across the sidewalk. I jumped at every sound I heard. I had decided to go early so I wouldn't bump into Madison on the street, and had made it clear when I spoke to him on the phone that I would only see him in the psychiatrist's office.

With hesitancy, I looked around each corner expecting to see Madison, then I would walk on. I inspected the elevator before I entered it and the hallway on floor number three before I exited. The doctor's name printed next to the door told me I was at the right place. I felt a great relief knowing I was at the doctor's office, and I was safe.

I opened the door. There was Madison! He had also come early. My heart began beating rapidly—it felt like it would jump through my blouse. He tried to approach me, but I dodged him with each attempt he made to get near me. He was talking faster and faster, using all his powers of persuasion, his power over me. I put my hands over my ears and continued to back away from him.

Finally the door to the doctor's office opened. Dr. Booth asked us to come in. As I walked through the door, I noticed that the glass was a one-way mirror and knew that he'd kept us in that outer room so he could observe us.

"I've been watching your interaction," Dr. Booth stated calmly. "Now let's talk. I want to hear from each of you."

Madison tried to take the lead during the entire therapy time. "We must work on our relationship, must talk—we must live together so we can work through things." His argument sounded so logical, my heart was sinking as were any feelings of safety I'd had. I felt powerless and defenseless against him as the fear drew tighter and tighter around me.

Dr. Booth asked me a few questions and each time Madison started to answer for me. Dr. Booth noted this, and every time he ignored Madison. He then turned to me and again repeated the question and waited patiently until I could find the space, the words, and the courage to answer for myself. The doctor looked at me for a long time, studying me as one would study a cowering animal. The bruises on my face were still visible and the beating to my psyche had left me speaking slowly and timidly.

Finally Dr. Booth spoke. He looked straight at Madison. "So, you expect this woman to live with you after what you have done to her?"

"I—I've told her why I do it—so it should be all right."

A light went on—all my Psychology 101 flooded back to me: He's a psychopath, a pathological liar, and a sociopath, and he has no conscience. He thinks that if he explains why he beats and abuses me it makes it all right. Then he makes it my fault and everyone else's.

"No, you should not live together now," Dr. Booth continued. He abruptly told Madison that the time was up and asked him to leave.

After he ushered Madison out the door, Dr. Booth motioned for me to sit down and he closed the door. He formed his words slowly and carefully: "Your husband is a dangerous man. He will likely not stop his violence and you need to get away from him."

My eyes widened. How could he know that? What was he seeing about Madison's power and control that I'd been ignoring? For the first time I understood that there was more than fate at stake and that I truly *was* in danger.

"You also need help. I want you to promise to call me next week and I strongly suggest that you think about leaving New York."

I left the office. It was dark. The grasping shadows were even more desperately searching out every shape to grab and wrap their eerie fingers about. I stared to the right, then to the left, afraid they or something worse—like Madison—would grab me. Slowly I began to walk down the street toward the subway. Suddenly I heard footsteps behind me and before I could run, a hand reached out to grab my arm. Anyone but Madison, I thought, as I looked to see his pale green eyes.

"Honey, come home with me," he said desperately. "You can trust me—I'll make it up to you."

"No! No!" I shrieked as I pulled away.

He ran to the brick wall beside us and, like a madman, began banging his forehead against it. He turned back toward me so I could see the full effect of the blood seeping from his wounds, flowing downward through his eyebrows, and dripping slowly onto his cheeks. For an instant I knew that this insane man would kill me if I didn't react the way he wanted me to. My animal survival instincts had returned. His wounds weren't life-threatening to him, but they were to me if I didn't appear to care about them and him.

I put my arms around him. "Oh no, oh no, my darling," I said as I hailed a cab.

Once inside the cab I tried to instruct the driver to head toward Bellevue Hospital. Madison would think I was trying to get him to an emergency ward, but I knew they also had a psychiatric ward. But he would have none of it.

"I'm okay," he insisted, and then instructed the driver to take us to his apartment—our old apartment.

Now I knew I was completely trapped. He was stronger than I, both physically and mentally. The driver dropped us off in front of the dark brown building that I'd grown to hate and fear.

Once inside, Madison took possession of me again. He again became like a madman. "You are *mine!* I'll show you what you've always loved about me—the deep, passionate way I make love to you. I will make you moan again!"

He threw me on the bed, tearing at my clothes. Too afraid to fight back, too weak and tired to resist, I knew once again I was being raped. This time by my husband—this time by the man who could kill me.

As he entered me I moaned, then swallowed back the contents of my stomach as it rose in my throat. Surely he would kill me if he knew his lovemaking was causing me to throw up. I wanted to survive, so I moaned again. When he was finished he rolled over and went to sleep.

I lay there all night with my eyes open, listening for any sound that would tell me he was awake. I knew if I moved or if I tried to escape, it would wake him and he would kill me. I knew I had to wait until morning, and then tell him how much I loved him, how wonderful his lovemaking had been, and that I'd see him that evening at "our home" after work.

The plan was simple, but it was for survival. The next morning he seemed to believe me when I told him I wanted to take care of him forever, that I wanted to be his.

We walked out of the apartment together. I watched his pale green eyes stare at me, and I knew that he was wondering how far he could trust me. I forced a smile to slide across my face as I looked back at him, then let a lid fall slowly in a flirting wink. This assured him my old, flirtatious, obedient self was back and he turned to go to work and he waved. I waved back and walked away.

The Flashback

The mind ... It is dazzled when it emerges from its dark prison.

—PIERRE TEILHARD DE CHARDIN
The Phenomenon of Man

SPRING 1997, SEDONA, ARIZONA

I had written for days now. It was clear that the themes of power and control kept reappearing in my life. I stared out at the clouds rolling by Sedona's brilliant red rocks. The sun cast long shadows across the tall, red formations that reached like sentinels, hundreds of feet into the sky. I'd always thought that they looked like souls who'd been frozen in time so that over the years only the wind, and the rain that rarely came, would change their appearance.

I wondered what could cause a soul to have become frozen in the first place. Maybe they, like me hadn't faced their feelings and had become caught in their patterns of the past, thus sealing themselves into silent, stoic pillars.

The sun cast its last rays over the rock sentinels, and their warm, red tones made them look alive. This was my favorite time of day. My eyes filled with tears and I felt a drop fall over my lid and down my cheek, reminding me of the many tears I'd shed through the years. But even more, it made me think back to the first time, nearly twenty years ago, when I knew I must look into the struggle for power and try to connect the dots of the strange events of my life.

I was living along the California coast and had left my student days, Germany, and Madison behind many years before. Though my portrait career and reputation had continued to grow, traveling had become my nemesis. It had taken me all over the world, often aimlessly, never quite knowing what I was looking for.

I'd been living for years with the occasional strange phenomenon of marble walls turning to rough stone blocks, black pumps turning to leather boots and my hands for moments transforming into large, strong, male hands.

Then, strangely and for no seemingly apparent reason, my eyes had started to water excessively. When this happened, they felt like they were floating in lukewarm, velvety liquid. This also continued for years until I felt I could no longer keep my sanity if I did not figure out why.

So that's when I decided to go to Hawaii to see my good friend, Leilani, my soul sister in the search for the meaning of it all.

LATE 1977, HONOLULU, HAWAII

Leilani, only five feet, with a graceful body, golden skin, dark eyes and hair, was a great contrast to my five-foot-five, fair skin, and blond hair. Men often turned to follow us with their eyes as Leilani and I walked together.

When Leilani and I weren't out playing together, we would sit and share our thoughts, our dreams, and our search for the meaning of life. At those times, the rest of the world receded around us.

I was hoping, this time, Leilani would be able to help me find a way to overcome these reality-shattering, time-shifting happenings that had been occurring over these last years, especially now that they grew worse every day. It was my eyes that were the most annoying phenomenon—that awful feeling that they were floating in a tepid, velvety liquid. And whenever it happened I would become extremely disoriented, everything would blur, and for a brief while I couldn't function normally. More and more I was afraid to go anywhere in case it happened while I was driving. And, most frightening of all, sometimes I couldn't remember who I was while I was in this space between the past and the present.

Leilani was happy to see me. She put a fragrant *pikake lei*, our favorite, around my neck and hustled me to her waiting Mercedes.

Shortly, we were both talking as if no time had passed since we'd seen each other. Leilani listened carefully as I told her more about the ever-increasing phenomenon with my eyes. Soon we were venturing further into a general discussion of the possibilities of reincarnation.

"You know, Marilyn, I have such a cross section of beliefs—you should try it. At least in my Eastern and Hawaiian beliefs I can feel reincarnation is so. It's only in the Christian I have to fight off the demon of disbelief."

"Well, I'm sure there's something in all of this I'm supposed to learn. Otherwise, why would I have had such a bad marriage? I lost all my confidence during that time and also gave all my power to another person. I must have some deep power issues and it feels like they're more than just from my childhood."

"And you don't inherit powerlessness through the genes," Leilani added with a chuckle.

Her last statement made me laugh and I could tell she was being especially sensitive to me and to what I was sharing since she was having one of her own dilemmas: the hauntings in her house had become more frequent and were affecting her family.

Several times her sons had run into her room in the middle of the night, terrified that something was in their bedroom and trying to attack them. Leilani's ex-husband, a philosophy professor who operated entirely from his intellect and had trouble changing a light bulb, had stayed over one night and panicked when he saw a cloud float through the guest room above his head. He did not stay over again.

"Marilyn, I've got to find out what is going on. It's affecting my children, my work, my whole life." I nodded and was trying to understand how she felt. Leilani went on, "I've gone to the priest of my church, and can you believe it? He told me to forget it. He acted like I was making it up. All he seemed concerned about was the fact that I'd kicked my husband out. He told me I should say a few Hail Marys and perhaps I'd be forgiven." Leilani's fist hit the table between us. "The church hasn't helped me at all with this!"

"Maybe you should see Papa Doc, the Hawaiian priest, the Kahuna you told me about."

"No, no, I don't want to think the hauntings have anything to do with Hawaiian beliefs!" Leilani said, clearly very distressed.

"Well, I pushed on, "maybe you should look at it, Leilani. You might be living in a house that's been built on sacred Hawaiian land. And I've never told you this, but I've met the previous owners and they really appeared to have some screws loose—like they had some deep, dark malady or something. You could at least have the house blessed."

"Marilyn, I want to handle this another way for now. I've heard of a meditation group that can take you back to the root of a problem. Maybe it would work for you, too."

I was becoming desperate to find some answers and so I nodded and agreed to go to the meditation meeting the next evening.

Leilani and I met outside the auditorium at 7:00 P.M. As we entered the hall the meeting was about to begin. Nearly all the seats were already taken so we slipped into some chairs near the rear.

"I want each of you to find some physical symptom that you want to concentrate on," the instructor began. "It can be something that's been very bothersome that you feel you're ready to know the truth about."

Well, that was easy. The velvety liquid that formed around my eyes and caused my disorientation—that's what I wanted to know about. Maybe knowing that would open the truth to the changing corridors, the leather boots, and to my hands becoming male hands.

"Do each of you have your symptoms well in mind?"

There was the energized silence of a room full of expectant participants.

The instructor's voice began at a slow, hypnotic pace. "You will start by taking a deep breath and relaxing." I sat back and started to follow the instructions. The instructor's voice droned on and on, suggesting we relax first the right foot, then the left. He then proceeded to give these same suggestions of relaxation for the entire body. He paused, then went on with emphasis, "Now, it is very important, if you want to know the truth, that you give permission for it to emerge from within you. You, and only you, can say yes or no to allowing the whole truth, whatever it is, to appear.

His voice set a slower pace. "Relax—you are relaxing more and more, going deeper and deeper." He paused. "At this point I want you to concentrate on the physical symptom you have chosen. Do you want to give permission to knowing the truth? Say yes or no."

I mumbled, "Yes," as I felt the warm liquid start flowing around my eyes.

Suddenly I was—where? I tried to raise my hands. My fingers throbbed in pain. My arms were leaden and aching. I looked down to see heavy leather straps laced over my arms and holding them to a rough, wooden chair arm. I struggled to free myself from the confining restraints. I stopped when I realized it was hopeless to try to break the thick bindings that held my frail, thin, raw hands. My long, slender fingers gripped desperately at the plank of the arm rest.

Suddenly I felt someone jab me with a hot poker and my body jerked in torturous response.

Pain echoed through me. My head lurched forward to my chest. My dazed, tearing eyes moved down over my rough hemp gown, then fell to the floor where a blood-red triangle of light glowed at my feet. With deep resolve, I raised my head and followed the twisting light to its source. A dark oak cross hung from the wall and nearly covered a deep-red stained glass window. A light poured through only the lower left side of the window, and was cut neatly by the dark cross, thus forming the shape of a triangle as the light twisted downward.

I looked up from the blood-red triangle and saw pale green eyes staring at me—threatening, hostile, and angry eyes. I knew instinctively that they were the eyes of the Inquisitor. He wore a long, black robe and held a glowing poker menacingly near my head where my brown hair had been recently shorn so there was now only a close crop of new growth.

For a moment my mind wanted to flee back to the safety of being a blond artist in another time, but then I remembered I'd asked for the truth—and had given permission to be shown all the truth about the warm, velvety liquid that formed around my eyes.

Somehow, oddly, a calm settled over me. I was not afraid of this Inquisitor. With inner knowing, I knew I was a female monk, and that I often disguised myself as a man so I could travel more safely as I went from country to country sharing healing and psychic predictions. I wrote verses and quadrangles that touched many people; I loved the written word more than the spoken.

The Inquisitor waved the hot poker in front of my eyes. I stared back at his menacing green eyes, which were darkening with jealousy and hatred. Eyes met eyes for a seeming eternity. My intuitive psychic powers drove into his eyes, casting fear into them—cold, animal fear.

But then the control snapped, and in quick barbarous gestures of fury, the Inquisitor shoved the steaming, crimson poker at me. It caught me at the side of my head, behind my eyes, and began to loosen them from their sockets. I felt the warm, sticky blood flow around my eye sockets and pour down over my cheeks as the Inquisitor gouged my eyes from my head.

"You coward, you heathen, you despicable devil," I yelled. "You know I have my powers in my eyes, you know they could overtake you, that my powers are stronger that yours. You are afraid of them."

A sharp pain hit my chest and a fire bored deep into my heart. Then I felt a dark, quiet, peacefulness descend over me and soon all was quiet.

"Ten—nine—eight, you are waking up, coming back into the room. Seven—six—five—four, you are awake and alert, feeling good and remembering all you've experienced. Three—two—one, touch the chair, feel the floor under your feet." The instructor paused, then said, "Does anyone want to share their experience?"

I sat stunned. I hadn't found rough stone walls and corridors. I hadn't found my hands as a strong man's hands as had happened so often in my disorienting experiences. I'd found frail, female hands. Where had I been? Had this really happened? Had I gone back in time? Do we *really* have other lives? I must have found a different lifetime, a lifetime *where I'd been in the Inquisition, and where I'd died.* My hair was brown, not blond, and had been shorn from my head. I'd had my eyes gouged out by someone afraid of me and my powers. Why was I killed? Had I misused my powers? Was this why I always make myself powerless *now*, so I won't be killed? I hadn't answered anything. I'd only raised even more questions.

Days later I tried to tell Leilani about my painful, confusing dilemma, but she had slipped more deeply into her own troubles. She was even more disturbed by her own haunting experience— and confused about where to seek help from any of her beliefs: Eastern superstition, Christian dogma, or Hawaiian lore.

One night, since we'd last talked, Leilani had looked out the window and had seen the Hawaiian Night Stalkers, the sacred ghost warriors of another dimension, walking through her yard. Most Hawaiians were terrified of the Night Stalkers and believed they meant death to anyone in the third dimension who saw them. Leilani told me of this and said it didn't fit with her Christian beliefs and she was going to disregard it even though the haunting incidents in her house had increased. I could see the terror in her eyes and could tell she was now mixing her beliefs in a fearful knot, trying desperately to find a solution.

I ended up listening to her story and burying mine more deeply.

Two weeks passed before I realized that something was missing: I no longer had the feeling that my eyes were floating in liquid.

* * *

Apollo's nudging against my leg pulled me back from my reverie of the past. It was dark outside. I was still standing at the window, staring out at the darkened red rocks. Apollo brushed against me, letting me know that he needed to go for a walk. I scratched his little black head, put his leash on him, and we walked out under the splendor of the Arizona stars.

The search into this strange, bizarre phenomenon of slipping back into my past life at the Inquisition would have to wait. "Apollo, when we get back, it's time for me to go back to my writing and finish up with my marriage to Madison. You *would not* have liked him."

Apollo growled.

Chapter Nine

The Ticket

For when we dare not hope for change, we lose even the desire for it.

—GAIL SHEEHY
Pathfinders

WINTER 1959, NEW YORK

I constantly looked over my shoulder whenever I walked anywhere in New York.

Every day after work I left the Saks Fifth Avenue department store by a different door when returning home to my little room. The store was a block square and had guards posted at most doors, so my fear was somewhat lessened.

Julie and Scott met me once a week. I always insisted we click our glasses so I could toast my once-a-week luxury, a single martini— two olives. I never really let on how afraid I was, but was sure I didn't fool them. They insisted I not tell them where I lived so Madison would have no way of getting that information from them. They were terrified that he might call them, stalk them, or beat my address out of them.

I could afford one meal a day at the employee's cafe. I would pile my plate high with the least expensive pastas and potato dishes. Here I was, a college graduate, and I could only get a job as a department store salesgirl with a take-home pay of $26.00 a week. Even though the country was in a recession, I felt that all my dreams were gone and that I was a failure. The brutal wounds on my face began to heal, but those in my heart only deepened.

One day, my supervisor came over to my counter. "Marilyn," she said, "there's someone here to see you." My heart pounded as I turned and came face-to-face with Madison.

"I have to talk to you," he said plainly. Though my pulse beat hard in my ears, I thought there was some safety in speaking to him at work with so many people around.

Madison walked to the door of the stock room. I followed. His hand shot out, grabbing me, tearing painfully into my forearm as he pulled me through the door.

His fists tore into my face. I screamed. Three guards had to remove him from my battered and bruised body lying on the stock room floor. I knew that someday Madison would kill me if I couldn't keep him from finding me.

Prior to this my pride had not allowed me to ask anyone, besides Julie and Scott, for help. I'd always distanced myself from my parents so I had not written them about what was going on in my marriage. I knew now it was time to admit I needed them and so I called.

"Mom, I need help."

They immediately called my Uncle Llewellyn and the next day he arrived in New York. A tall, elegant man, he often acted as the wise mentor of our family, since he was a successful writer and a world traveler.

I met him at his hotel room. His eyes surveyed me thoroughly. I knew my bruises were apparent to him, but he did not let on.

"Marilyn, I'm glad you called your parents. Since we never heard from you, none of us had any idea you were having a problem with your marriage. Let's find a solution," he said, his eyes piercing directly into me. Noticing my discomfort, he added, "But first let's have lunch."

The menu was a blur. When I could make out the words, I had trouble knowing what they meant. Uncle Llewellyn recognized I was suffering from what is now known as the *battered wife syndrome*, and saw that I was unable to make a decision—any decision, and he ordered for me.

The last beating had broken my spirit, just as the first one had broken my nose. When I could speak at all it was slow and halting.

I wasn't yet aware that there was an old, deep pattern of power-lessness within me from other lifetimes, nor that the forgotten pattern had been reawakened when I met Madison.

I had lost the concept of being in control of my own fate and thought it was my fate to be with Madison, that I was to be controlled by him until I could flee—then again be drawn back to him—back and forth, perhaps never to truly get away from him. I felt I still loved him and I was not sure I could ever make myself leave him permanently.

"That's what the rest of my life will be," I told Uncle Llewellyn. His puzzled, pained look prompted me to go on. "I still love him. Yes, someday he will probably kill me."

Later in his hotel room, Llewellyn pulled a large yellow tablet from his briefcase. He drew a line down the center of the page and said, "We will list why you should leave him on the left and why you should stay with him on the right."

I sat still for a long while. "How can I leave him for good? I love him!" I said through the muddle of a beaten mind. "I *need* him, he needs *me!*" My thoughts raced wildly, trying to find a solution, yet always dodging the pattern of powerlessness. Finally, with Llewellyn's prompting, I made the list. The entries grew quite long under the leaving column. I could only come up with, "I love him and he needs me," under the staying column.

I sat quietly for a long time, then finally I mumbled, "I don't know."

Llewellyn rose from the chair to his full six feet, two inches and announced: "Marilyn, I have an airline ticket with your name on it. The flight leaves New York this evening. I will loan you what you need until you find a job and can start over. You have fifteen minutes to decide. In the meantime, I'm going to pack my things and get ready to catch my plane back home."

It took me only moments to realize that my decision would determine whether I would live. I knew Llewellyn would never come back for me again. Like a small, defeated animal, I walked toward him and put out my hand. He placed the airline ticket to Minnesota into it.

Chapter Ten

The Loft

*. . . each of us is limited only by our trust and belief systems.
If we are willing to risk, the gains are so staggering that
we wonder, as we enter the process of initiation, why did it
take us so long to begin?*

—GORDON-MICHAEL SCALLION
Scallion Newsletter

*WINTER 1959, **THE FARM IN MINNESOTA***

Dustin sat with the rifle across his lap. We both trembled, waiting
for a door to burst open, a window to shatter.

Only days before, I'd arrived home, but not to a hero's welcome.
Divorce just didn't happen in my family. I wore my battle scars; that
made me tolerable.

I told my family only enough of what had happened to satisfy
their curiosity and to justify leaving my husband. The bruises that
were still there verified my story. We had no idea if Madison was
looking for me, but it was very likely.

My parents had long-standing plans to go to a community function. They had asked me to go with them, but with my battle scars

still visible, I in no way felt like being on display at a local gathering, so I told them they should go ahead without me.

"Anyway," I added half jokingly, "Dustin will protect me." I was sure Dustin, my seventeen-year-old brother, would take the job seriously. So after again assuring them I would be all right, they reluctantly agreed to go on to their meeting.

"Do *not* open the door to anyone, and do *not* answer the phone," they said as they walked out the door.

Dustin was in the bathroom when the phone rang. For a moment I forgot my parents' admonition, and I answered the phone.

"Hello? Marilyn, Marilyn, it's you!" It was Madison's voice.

I tried to disguise my voice, but it was too late.

"Marilyn, honey, I've got to talk to you. I'm coming now, to see you."

"No, Marilyn's not here." I hung up the phone, my hand shaking. But I knew it was no use. He had recognized my voice and now he knew where I was.

Dustin ran and grabbed the rifle and he and I just sat there the rest of the evening. He put the rifle across his legs. My kid brother, my protector. We didn't know if Madison's call had come from five miles away or five thousand.

I knew then that I would have to go into hiding. And when my parents came home that night, they knew it, too. The next day we packed my few things, they drove me to Minneapolis, and I disappeared into the streets of the city.

I rented a small room in an apartment building and looked for work. One night as I returned from a particularly late interview, I felt someone approach me on my right side, quickly followed by someone on my left. Fear gripped and surrounded me just as the men did, one on each side of me. They took my arms and began propelling me along between them.

"Do you think about running through the snow barefoot?" one said. Something that no one, *no one* could know about except Madison.

The other man said even more intimate things, again things that only Madison could've known. "Do you like honeymooning in Paris? Do you like to make love while cats make love?" They had been sent by Madison; he had hired them to find me—and now they had.

"Please, please let me go," I pleaded. "Please, please let me run away again! See these bruises, these marks? This is what he did to me. He will do it again—and he will *kill* me. Please give me just two hours before you tell him where I am." As silently as they had approached, they slipped away, first from one side, then from the other, but the panic and fear did not slip away.

I raced back to my room and threw things into a suitcase as quickly as I could. It didn't matter where I was going, I only knew I had to get away. I gathered the little money I had and ran deeper into the inner city. Clearly the two men had given me time to get away.

Now I knew if I were to live, I had to start over again, I had to delve into all the horrors of my time in Germany, the visit to the concentration camp, Hans and his menacing, diabolical laughter, Madison's beatings, and everything else that had happened to me. I needed to look at it all if I wanted to live. But I was not sure I knew how to search into it all—or that I really wanted to live.

I found a large room in a building that was dark and pock-marked like so many I'd seen in war-torn Europe. I wrote a name on the rental form in big block letters. JANE DOE—RITY, adding those last four letters so the alias wouldn't be so obvious.

I went to the library and checked out all the books I could find on World War II, including *The Story of Anne Frank*. I returned to my room and started to read the story of her family's confinement in the loft, hiding from the Gestapo.

Someone had also given me the book, *A Doll's House*. It was macabre and disgusting and I was terrorized as well as repelled by the diary account of a fourteen-year-old girl forced into prostitution for the soldiers at a concentration camp. Not only did I relate to it, I *became* the girl in *A Doll's House*. I thought of Hans, an S. S. Captain, standing there at the door, looking at my battered face, my partially bald head, and laughing, doubling over in laughter over my pain and my wounds. How could he do that? What kind of animal was he? I let my mind race over the possible answers, and then from somewhere deep inside me came the truth, the knowing.

Hans had gone into the army when he was only a young man. Possibly he'd been a loving, tender child. I like to think we each start out that way, but then he'd become one of *Hitler's Youth*, and he was taught, he was very carefully taught and trained. Trained to march, to fight, and to laugh at others' misery. And as I had now read, most of the S.S. were the keepers of the concentration camps. Hans had risen to the rank of captain, so certainly he must have proven he was a good soldier, must have done his job well. He had been trained to kill and had been trained to be amused by that killing and the pain and suffering that went with it. He had been trained to separate himself from those who were suffering—from *them*—and when I walked through the door with my battered face, I became one of *them.*

Now I understood what had happened that night in Germany, why Hans had laughed at my battered face, but it didn't hurt any less.

The pain and what I was learning from my readings about World War II drew around me like a darkening legion of gloom. I didn't know how or if I could go on. One day shortly thereafter, I entered my room and drew all the shades, blocking out all light. My small bed stood in the corner against the wall, reminding me of the bunks I'd seen in Dachau. Wearily, I sat down on the bed. I pulled my legs up close to my body, in a fetal position, and started to rock back and forth, over and over, thinking about everything I'd seen, everything I'd read, and everything that had happened to me.

My cold fingers traced the sunken right side of my nose where Madison had broken it. I felt the sharp, bony ridge across my cheek where it had been shattered. I let my hands slip to the top of my head to feel the short hairs growing out. Hot tears rolled down my face. They tasted sour and salty and anguished.

I don't know how many days I rocked, curled up in that corner, staring at the door. The room had become my own loft, my own hiding place. I was waiting for *them* to come, waiting for the *Polizei*— the Gestapo—the S. S. Waiting for their pulsing siren, waiting for them to break down the door, and for their shiny black boots to march toward me. In my mind I was back in Nazi Germany.

All the horror of Germany and the beatings rolled together within me, awash in a sea of despair. I became the hunted. Swastikas, black boots, triangles, and pale green eyes all marched endlessly before me. Finally I thought I was going to die—I wanted to die—then I wasn't sure if I was dead already. Finally my mind snapped.

The snap could have led me to suicide, or it could have pushed me over the edge and into insanity, but instead the resounding snap deadened my grasping need for knowing and steered me back to reality. I pushed back the soiled, sweat-covered linens that were wrapped tightly around my body. I had sat for hours holding my legs, hugging them close as if they were the body of a child. Tears had streaked my face and I smelled of vomit and urine and the sweat of fear.

Maybe I understood what had happened to me, maybe I understood what had happened in Nazi Germany, and maybe I did not. I threw back the curtains, strode to the door which, only hours before, had been the door the S. S. Captain would storm through. On shaky, feeble legs I walked into the daylight. I heard a bird's song warbling above me, saw a butterfly rise from a flower, and knew that I, like the butterfly, had just broken from my cocoon.

I came out of hiding long enough to file for divorce. Uncle Llewellyn flew in and arranged for an old family friend, a lawyer, to handle the divorce.

Papers could not be served on Madison since we had no address for him, so my lawyer arranged for a notice to appear in a New York newspaper. This was the last known city he'd lived in and therefore, it satisfied the legal requirements. My lawyer was right—it was a very simple procedure. I couldn't bring witnesses from Germany, nor did I want to involve Julie and Scott. My bruises still showed, so we filed for an uncontested divorce, asking for no alimony or support, and, of course, there was no need for child support.

My lawyer had also done a background check on Madison. "You're very lucky," he said. "You probably don't know it, but you're his third wife. And he had battered them *all*."

I was furious. "I want to send him to prison," I yelled.

"No, no," the lawyer advised. "It would be difficult to convict him without witnesses, and even if you could, he would only get a year or two and it would be *you* he'd be looking for when he came out. The others fled to save their lives and I suggest you do the same."

I protested, "But he tried to murder me—he tried to murder *them*—what if he succeeds the next time? I'll feel terrible if he murders someone."

The lawyer looked at me and shook his head, "That someone could be you. If you even try to take him to court for attempted murder, you'll be looking over your shoulder for the rest of your life."

I left his office and went back into hiding.

Large, fluffy snowflakes fell as I packed my few belongings into the small Volkswagen I'd bought.

I went back into the apartment and walked to the round aquarium that had helped me keep my sanity during the last few months. I dipped the net into the water and pulled out my pet snail. He'd grown huge after he'd killed my fish by eating all their food.

I carried him down the hall and out the back door to a small, nearby pond. I released him from his bondage. I didn't know if he'd survive. I didn't know if *I* would survive.

I took the small rattan monkey that hung from my rear-view mirror and gave to a little child I saw passing by on the street.

"What's its name?" she asked.

"Madison," I said as I turned and walked away. I only briefly glanced back at the dark grey building that had been my home for the last seven months.

I climbed behind the wheel and began to drive south. Like the birds, I thought, leaving the cold and heading south for the winter. Maybe I'll find some sunshine, maybe I'll *become* Sunshine again.

The In-Between Years

Many of the next years were aimless, as I traveled from place to place. I kept gathering new friends—and just kept dancing on the wheel of life as if everything was all right.

My career kept growing. I received more and more recognition for my portraits.

But it didn't give me the identity I needed, the self I'd lost.

P_{ART} II

Lost in the Acting

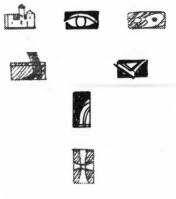

*C*hapter Eleven

The Kiss

Time has no meaning when you're in a timeless place ...

SHORTLY AFTER THE IN-BETWEEN YEARS, HONOLULU, HAWAII

Demanding lips pressed against mine. White flashes of passion surged through my body. Waves of heat began at my thighs and rippled upward as my knees weakened. I returned the kiss and waited for what I thought would come next.

Leilani was having one of her fabulous parties. She always gathered people from all over the world. Tonight she threw a catered feast aboard one of her friends' sixty-foot yacht.

Dozens of people were milling about the polished deck. I gripped my glass of champagne and walked around, meeting people. It was always hard for me to do that though most people never knew it. I always presented the side of me that loved to laugh and play and never let them see the true shyness I felt inside, nor the fact that I always held most of myself back.

I was wondering if Leilani had her usual string of single men at the party when my eyes caught a very unusual-looking woman. She had pale green eyes. Something about her seemed very familiar and

I felt I should know her. She noticed me looking at her so I looked away.

As the waiter poured me another glass of champagne, I introduced myself to two men standing by the bar. They were both charming and we chatted for awhile. Inside I held myself distant though I smiled and flirted with one of them in particular. He took this as a sign he could corner all of my attention and when he began to get quite aggressive, I knew it had gone too far. I excused myself, thinking it best to get away and went to find the stairs that would lead down to the ladies' room.

I was unaware that anyone was following me.

I walked down the steps and when I reached the bottom, I opened a door. The room was pitch black, but once inside, I could see by the light from the doorway that I was in the yacht's huge master bedroom. I walked across the thick-carpeted room and opened the door to the master bath.

A few minutes later, as I left the bathroom and stepped back into the darkness, I felt two hands clasp my shoulders, turn me around and pull me toward them. Lips pressed against mine. I was alarmed and tried to resist but a strange, sensual feeling started to flow through me.

I didn't know who was kissing me, but I knew it was not the kiss of an attacker. It was soft and sensuous, even though it was demanding, and I soon found myself returning it, desiring more. I had never felt a kiss like that before. A passion started rising in me that set my whole body on fire. It felt like electrical charges were surging through my entire being.

Then as quickly as the hands had grabbed me, they released me, leaving me standing there in frustration. I could barely hear the footsteps as the mystery person crossed the room and walked to the door leading up to the deck. I heard the door open. Then by the light from the stairway, I saw who it was: *the woman with the pale green eyes.*

The door closed behind her and I stared into the darkness in disbelief. *The kiss had been from a woman.*

It took me a long time to compose myself enough to walk back up the stairs. As I crossed the deck, I was sure everyone was staring at me. I knew my face was red and I felt like I was burning up, no longer from passion but from embarrassment. Did what had just happened to me show?

The mystery woman's pale green eyes followed me as I walked across the deck. My insides trembled and I tried not to look at her, but something drew my eyes to meet hers. Her eyes penetrated into my soul with an arrogant invasiveness. I felt naked and exposed and was sure she knew how her kiss had affected me. I tried to look away, but I could not. I seemed unexplainably drawn to her.

She wore a pale pink blouse with a large lapel that formed a triangle pointing downward from her chin. There was something *familiar* about her, as if she reminded me of something or someone. I tried to remember what or who, but I couldn't grasp the memory that seemed to wisp away just like spider webs do when they're caught by the wind.

She was with another woman and they seemed to laugh a great deal together. I noticed their hands touched often.

She came toward me, and her pale green eyes pierced so intimately into me that I was sure they exposed my trembling. "My friend and I would like to meet you," she said with a firm voice. "We're both professional women and have just moved to Honolulu. My name's Tanya Stanford, and this is Cheri Prichard."

She reached for my hand. As she held it, electrical sparks started surging through me again as they had during the kiss. I knew I was turning red from a passion more profound than any I'd ever known. For lingering moments after the handshake, we stood there as if in a time warp. My mind felt drugged. "Why is this happening to me?'

With great effort, I was able to form words that I allowed to exit slowly with my breath. "I'm Marilyn Sunderman. I've just moved here also." The words started to come more easily as I went on. "I love the islands—I've been coming here for years."

"Then maybe you'd show us around," she purred, and said it so directly it was more a statement than a question.

I knew I really wanted to see her again, even felt I must see her again. I felt my face flush and I stammered, "Yes, yes, I could do that."

Tanya, Cheri, and I met often, always out somewhere, never at my place or theirs.

I began showing them the islands I loved so much: the thick, moist, tropical forests that led up to the Pali; the deep blue-greens of the windward side of the mountains that crossed Oahu; and the shoreline around the island where the soft white sand of the beaches met the lapping, azure-blue water. As we strolled along the shore, the tradewinds grabbed our laughter and carried it far out over the white-capped ocean.

I treasured our time together, though mostly it was for the chance to be with Tanya. There was never a mention about the kiss, so I tried to put it out of my mind or think of it as a mistake. But still the feeling lingered that somehow, from another time or place, I knew her.

One day as we passed by the flower-laden Niu Valley, I mentioned, "My home is in that valley." Tanya turned toward me, her eyes staring into me so deeply I had to hold tightly to the steering wheel to keep from trembling.

The next day the doorbell rang. It was Tanya. "I was out driving in the area. Can I come in?" She didn't wait for me to answer—she just walked in!

She had carefully fixed her light brown hair so that it framed her angular, square-jawed face just so. It had also been sprayed heavily so it wouldn't be blown out of place by the tradewinds. She wore off-white pants and a soft pink silk blouse. A single strand of perfectly matched pearls cascaded gently over her breasts. It was clear she had taken great care in dressing.

She proceeded to go from room to room, acting as if she were having her own déjà vu experience and knew where everything was—just as if she'd been there before, as if it might have been her home.

Tanya went to the sofa in the sun room and sat down. She motioned for me to sit next to her.

"I really want to get to know *you*, not things," she said. "Don't tell me anything about yourself, let's just be together." No one had ever said anything like that to me before; they'd always wanted to know about things, and what I did for a living. I liked her directness and sophistication. We began to talk about nothing special, we just talked. All the while she kept her pale green eyes on me—I could feel the flush rising from my neck and engulfing my face.

As her eyes penetrated into me, I was flooded by the awareness of their familiarity.

She leaned forward and set her glass of wine on the table. She pulled her hand back, then let her fingers lightly touch the top of my fingers.

Bombastic sparks, more colorful than fireworks, raced through me. I knew I was turning deep red. I felt on fire.

She put her hands on my shoulders and pulled me toward her. She urgently, yet softly, pressed her lips against mine. Flashes of passion surged through me. She pressed harder against my mouth as she continued her kiss. Her tongue spread my lips and gently entered me.

She took my hand, wrapping her fingers around mine, and led me back toward my bedroom as if it were not the first time she'd done that.

While she was making love to me she whispered, "I love you."

Chapter Twelve

Azure-Blue Water

Several months before the party on the yacht where I met Tanya, Leilani called me, terribly distraught, and begged me to come to Hawaii.

"It's getting worse at my house. The haunting is beginning to consume me. When can you come to Honolulu?" she pleaded.

"I'm scheduled for Mrs. Wong's portrait sitting in a week, but I could come sooner," I told her. "I can come now."

"Yes, yes. Thank you!" she said with relief.

I'd heard the desperation in her voice. I went in and packed my bags.

I drove from my California home toward the Los Angeles airport, taking the coastal route. I wanted to look at the deep green waves crashing along the shoreline, and I wanted to think about the blue waters of the Islands. I loved Hawaii so much, and was glad that I'd soon be there.

A seagull swooped down from the clouds and dove toward the murky water. I wondered why she flew there when she could be over Hawaii where the water was azure-blue.

* * *

We got into Leilani's car at the Honolulu airport and again, she had brought me our favorite *pikake lei*. She immediately started talking excitedly about the latest incidents at her house. "I've seen the Night Stalkers again. They were carrying torches and were chanting. They paraded across my backyard."

This was the second time Leilani told me about seeing the Night Stalkers. I hadn't thought much of it the first time she'd mentioned it, but this time I was alarmed.

I thought back to what I'd heard about the Night Stalkers: they were Hawaiian Ghost Warriors, had their own territory in another dimension that paralleled ours, and usually co-existed peacefully with us. The Hawaiian people considered them sacred since they existed to protect the land. But what caused my alarm was that I'd heard that if anyone ever saw the Night Stalkers, they would die!

"Did anyone else see them?" I asked as calmly as I could, not trying to betray my concern.

"No, no one else has seen them," she replied. "But they're real. I know they are. And worse—" she broke off, "and worse, when I went under the house I found writing on the pillars."

Leilani's house was built on a hill and had huge pillars holding up the front since the lot was so sloped.

"What did it say?" I asked cautiously but calmly, hoping some of my calm would pass on to Leilani. It seemed to have no effect.

"I was looking for my poodle, Misty," Leilani went on excitedly. "I'd never been under the house before. The rafters and pillars were all streaked with dark, black paint scribbles—like symbols or signs. I don't know what they mean, but I do understand the words: *THIS HOUSE IS DAMNED!*"

Leilani's words rang in my ears and touched a memory. Several years before Leilani had bought the house, I'd been at a party in Honolulu and had met the couple she'd bought it from. They'd invited me to have cocktails the next evening.

When I went to their house that next night, their behavior had alarmed me. It started when I approached the house and heard a droning chant coming from beneath the house. Then as I entered, I was surrounded by black walls. The only source of light was a flickering fire in the center of the room. It cast a dancing pattern across some strange markings that had been painted on the walls.

The discomfort I was feeling with the whole scene worsened when the hostess approached me and offered me something from a black, skull-shaped bowl, a bowl covered with the same markings as were on the walls.

"I think I've made a mistake," I said, declining the drugs in the bowl. "I must be going." I fled out the door.

A macabre, mosaic puzzle was forming in my mind as I remembered that evening, and Leilani's whispered words were driving the final pieces into place. I was convinced they'd been Satan worshipers, that it was their symbols on the rafters, and that they'd scrawled the words: THIS HOUSE IS DAMNED! It'd been these worshipers of evil who had drawn the Night Stalkers to this property—to do their job and protect it from these worshipers of the darkness.

Leilani and I talked for hours. I really had no answers, but I told her what I could piece together of the puzzle.

"Maybe that's why I got the house for so little," Leilani said frantically. "They were fleeing from it!"

I tried to tell her that everything would be all right, though I wasn't sure it would be.

"I'm going to have the house blessed—exorcised—I'll have everything done to it," Leilani finally said.

It was on that day that I decided to stay in Honolulu—to move there. I loved it there, Leilani needed me, and besides, I had Mrs. Wong's portrait to do.

Leilani owned a very successful real estate firm. I asked her to find me a home. "Something in a valley," I suggested.

Chapter Thirteen

Mrs. Wong's Portrait

Vision is the art of seeing things invisible.
—JONATHAN SWIFT
Thoughts on Various Subjects from Miscellanies

Leilani's call brought me to Honolulu a week early. I had been scheduled to fly there to do a portrait of Mrs. J. R. Wong, a woman from a noted Chinese family. The portrait was to help her celebrate her fiftieth birthday.

The portrait stood on the easel in front of me. I knew it was good, and it was nearly finished. I had caught her black hair blowing in the wind and her delicate, olive-toned skin.

When I'd met with Mrs. Wong, I followed the portrait procedure that I'd long ago found worked so well. I would spend time talking with a client until I had a sense of the person and then I would let it gel inside until I got a vision of how I was to do the portrait. Then I'd take photos to guide me during the weeks of work.

As had so often happened, the vision of Mrs. Wong's portrait came at an unexpected moment. I was driving along the shore toward my home. A gentle tradewinds breeze blew through my open window and sunlight splashed across the dashboard. I'd just driven by a tree covered with ginger blossoms and the breeze had caught their fragrance and sent it flowing through the open window and into my car. I thought about castles in Europe and how long it had been since I'd seen one, and then that reminded me of Mrs. Wong's regal bearing.

Though she was a shy, fragile person, she carried herself in a stiff, formal manner that appeared impenetrable. She had the bearing of a true Chinese matron from an old and established aristocracy. She had a job, but it was mostly to get out of the house. Her children were grown and rarely came around; they couldn't stand their father anymore, and they didn't understand why she stayed with him.

As I drove, I saw a vision of Mrs. Wong's painting blazoned across the windshield. I wanted to argue with wherever or whomever this picture had come from. The painting before my mind's eye showed Mrs. Wong, her hair blowing in the wind, and a long, bright mauve scarf fluttering behind her in the breeze. The colors around her were shocking pinks, mauves, and purples. What had happened to her formal stiffness? This image was all wrong, as were the colors; they would clash with her olive skin. And the shape of the canvas I saw in my mind was strange, too—36 inches wide and only 16 inches tall—it would be as if the canvas was flopped on its side. I'd never done a portrait like that. It just seemed all wrong.

Despite my objections, the vision persisted and grew even clearer. There was Mrs. Wong with her head thrown back and the wind blowing through her hair. A scarf was tied loosely around her neck, and as the wind caught the scarf, it blew it behind her, filling the entire length of the canvas, all 36 inches of it. It gave her a look of freedom and abandon.

From experience, I'd learned that whoever—whatever—gave me these visions usually won out. I could argue, but the vision almost always ended up the right way to do the portrait.

I called Mrs. Wong and told her I was ready for the next phase. "This will involve some posing and some photo-taking," I said.

"Can we do it at my hillside home?"

"Yes, I can come to your home," I told her. "That's a good idea."

When I arrived, I met Mr. Wong as he was going out the door. He was in a hurry and was very abrupt.

Through all my years of painting portraits I'd become quite accustomed to people sharing deep, intimate parts of their lives with me. It was as if they wanted me to know their secrets so I could fully know *them*.

"He's going to see his mistress," Mrs. Wong began. "The children tell me I should leave him, but I don't know what I would do on my own. I'm afraid to be alone." After telling me more about her entrapment, she told me she was having her portrait done for herself. She had always done things for the children, for her husband, for the ancestors. She bit gently on her lip, setting the bite tightly as she said, "This is for *me*."

"Then let's begin," I suggested. "Mrs. Wong, do you have an electric fan?"

"Yes."

"Do you have a long scarf?"

"Yes."

"Please bring me the fan and, if you would, please, tie the scarf loosely around your neck."

As I set up the fan, Mrs. Wong tied the scarf at her neck and sat down primly in her chair in front of me.

The wind of the fan caught her by surprise. She let out a joyous laugh as she threw her head backward; her hair blew in the wind and the scarf flew into a long trail behind her.

Fortunately, I had already adjusted my camera and I caught that spontaneous moment of laughter on film. It was just what I needed— and exactly what I'd seen in the vision.

I took four more rolls of film, mostly to satisfy Mrs. Wong that I was doing my job. I already knew that the very first photo had captured the essence of her as I'd seen in my vision.

I returned to my studio and started painting her portrait. As I painted, the portrait evolved magically, almost instantaneously.

I could not contain myself or wait to call Mrs. Wong. Only a few days had passed, but I knew I wanted to share it with her. I knew the portrait was good, and that it was nearly completed.

Mrs. Wong rang the bell at the door of my studio and walked in. I'd thought long and hard about the best way to present her portrait to her. I'd placed the painting on an easel near the entrance, so as she stepped through the door it would be the first thing she would see. She entered and there it was, the portrait of her on a canvas that was very wide but only 16 inches high.

She gasped when she first saw it. Then she stared at it intensely and in silence. I could feel that she was mentally shaking her head. Her eyes peered out from the narrow folds of her lids. Her lids widened slightly as she turned to me and said, "Is that me?"

"Yes," I said, "that is you."

Another long period of silence went by. I grew afraid that maybe this time I'd really blown it—maybe this time, I had my first unhappy client.

Finally, she turned back to me and mouthed the words, "I'm beautiful."

I looked at this woman who was realizing this perhaps for the first time and said, "Yes, you are."

She smiled, the same smile I'd painted in the portrait, and I knew that I had caught the true essence and soul of Mrs. Wong.

She stayed and stared at the portrait for a long, long time. As she left she said she'd be back in a couple of days for the final posing.

The door closed behind her and I knew there was not going to be a final posing. I knew the portrait was finished.

Mrs. Wong returned two days later at the appointed time, expecting a final posing session. I'd already signed the painting.

This time Mrs. Wong brought a friend. She walked through my door and waved her arms wildly as she said to her friend, "Look at me—look at me, I'm beautiful."

Her friend stared at the portrait and smiled in agreement. "Yes, yes, she caught you. She caught that special part of you that you only reveal when you are truly being yourself."

Mrs. Wong walked back and forth in front of her portrait. She couldn't contain herself. Like her portrait, she was animated, and alive, and vibrant—and she had the long scarf tied loosely around her neck.

Calming down, she approached me and said, "I looked at myself in the mirror last night and for the first time in my life, I said, 'I love you'. You have no idea what you have given me."

Mrs. Wong had become her portrait.

She called me months later to tell me that she was getting a divorce, and that at work she'd been promoted to manager of her department.

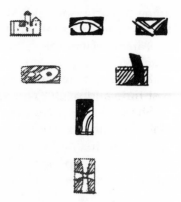

*C*hapter Fourteen

The Commitment

God never tells us in advance whether the course we are to
follow is the correct one.
                    —ALBERT EINSTEIN
                    Einstein, His Life and Times

Was my mind playing tricks on me, or had Tanya really said, "I love you"?

My body was on fire all the time. My mind was on vacation. I walked around in a daze. Wanting to be with Tanya had become an obsession and I wondered if it showed.

I'd always held the bigger part of myself in—ever since Madison. I was afraid of people knowing my feelings, especially now that I was walking on the edge and falling in love with a woman.

Tanya visited me again, and again it was very clear she had dressed herself carefully. A white silk blouse flowed gently down from her shoulders and over her breasts. A gold buckle with inlaid mother-of-pearl matched her gold and mother-of-pearl earrings. Within moments, she again led me to the bedroom. This time, it was my voice saying, "I love you." Tanya was silent.

We were lying there looking at one another. Tracing her finger along my arm, she said, "I want to play tour guide this time, I want to take you to Kauai for the weekend."

Tanya selected the romantic Coco Palms, a very Hawaiian-style hotel on one of the other islands. Set on the beach, the hotel also had a canal flowing through its grounds. I had never been there before, but I wasn't going to be much of a tourist. My mind was not on the swaying palms, but on the fire burning within me and the need to touch and be near this woman who felt so familiar.

On our first night, we went to the Polynesian show. All the while the fire dancer performed on the stage with his flaming swords, a similar flame was rising in my body, coursing through my veins and rising higher and higher. It was as if I had no control over it nor any control over my desire to be with Tanya.

After the show, Tanya suggested a walk along the waterway. I was still ablaze like the flaming swords we'd just seen. As we walked she took my hand. I was sure everyone was watching us, that *everyone would see us, that they would know we were lovers*. The thought terrified me.

"You know this is not what I want to be doing," I said. "I want to be near you but I don't want people to see us."

"Come," she said, pulling at my hand as we returned to the room.

I wasn't sure how much of what I felt was love or how much was the need to be near this woman who felt so familiar—the two had become so intertwined—but I did know that I was falling more and more desperately in love with Tanya. Nothing in my life had prepared me for what I was feeling.

How could this be happening to *me?* How could I feel this way about another woman? And always, there was the haunting familiarity, the feeling that I'd known those pale green eyes, this touch, *this* love, somewhere, someplace before. I felt it so strongly it seemed fated, a part of my destiny to meet this person and fall in love whether it was a man or a woman.

Back in Honolulu, Tanya visited me often. Always I said, " I love you." Always there was no reply. I wanted to hear the words so desperately, but I began to wonder if I'd really heard her say it that one time when we first made love.

One day while I was having lunch with Leilani, a hand came from behind and touched me on the shoulder. I could feel my face burning, the heat rising in my body, and I knew it was Tanya's hand.

"May I join you?" she asked, her pale green eyes piercing deep into my reddened face. I felt naked before her eyes.

Later Leilani took me aside and whisperingly said, "She's made love to you, hasn't she?" Her question jolted me and told me the answer to what I so feared: my loving a woman showed.

Love and passion seemed to consume me now. Whenever Tanya would wear the pink blouse with the large triangle lapel, I would catch myself trying to remember something, something about pink triangle bodices. Seeing her prismatic green eyes staring at me, I could almost hear the gasp escape from my throat. I was constantly searching to remember something.

Tanya was an unusual-looking woman. She had a firm, square jaw and very small features. Her eyes were narrow between her lids, but otherwise very wide and *very* green. It was a florid, almost olive, green that seemed to change often, as did her moods. She wore her brown hair shoulder length and teased it so it would fall around her face just so. She was always impeccably dressed. She wore her collars buttoned to the top, as if she was afraid to show any glimpse of flesh, or allow any scent to escape from her body. She often wore long, dark hose so she could cover her shapely legs and the fact that she never shaved them—or her underarms, for that matter. Thereby she could satisfy herself that she was a feminist, but still be closeted about it.

Tanya was truly an enigma. There is a place where saint and sinner must meet, the benevolent and the dictator, and it seemed that it was in Tanya. Almost anything you could say about her, you could also say the opposite: she was selfless, she was selfish; she was quiet, she needed center-stage; but always, she was impenetrable. She was a great interrogator of others but rarely, if ever, revealed anything about herself.

She'd spent most of her career as a hospital administrator. She belonged to many organizations that assisted the poor, the needy, the mentally and physically handicapped, and she'd become quite recognized for such work. Though sometimes she became quite child-like and appeared vulnerable, most of the time she was very controlling—not only of herself, but of everyone and everything around her. This bothered me; it reminded me of Madison's behavior, but I felt it would all be different because she was a woman.

It took some time for me to recognize that her desire to control and to be in charge was actually her defense against abandonment. Her father had abandoned her when she was a child and she was determined that no one would ever leave her again.

Her father had been an Episcopalian minister and in a moment of passion ran away with one of the women of the church. Her mother was so greatly humiliated that she died shortly thereafter.

Tanya's anger at her father turned to rage at his church, and she fled to the Catholic faith. There she found solace in the formal ceremonies of the High Mass and the strict rituals of the nuns. She would watch them as they walked in birdlike precision while going about their chores and she would try to imitate them in front of the large mirror at her aunt's house where she had gone to live after her mother died.

She was always trying to do good deeds. Deep inside she felt that if she couldn't save her father from his sins, she *would* at least save others.

Shortly before joining the convent with the goal of becoming a Mother Superior, Tanya met a young man from an old, established, and monied family. Who's to know if it was the thought of all the poor she could help with that very old money or if it was love? She chose to marry the young man instead of becoming a nun.

After a few years she found out that all that was left of the family's money was memories and she left her husband for a woman.

This caused a crack in her saintly persona and threatened her image of herself. By bumping into her shadow side, she found that she needed to hold herself even more tightly, needed to do even more good works.

Possibly because Tanya had come so close to being a nun, she carried herself like one. Somewhere I'd gotten the idea that she would be my salvation. I felt I had roamed aimlessly for years, having many lovers but never finding roots, seeking purpose but not even sure I had one. And then, I met Tanya. It seemed very important to know someone who seemed to be so in control, so in charge, so strong and clear in a purpose—doing good works. In fact, she was interested in saving people and I felt that I needed to be saved.

Tanya and I reached our first crossroads on a rainy afternoon. We walked to my bedroom and sat watching the rain glide down the large sliding glass door that led to my backyard. As she pushed me back on the bed, she said, "This must be our last time. I must stop seeing you." Sometimes I sobbed when I was being made love to, but my need to be with her had grown so great, I couldn't imagine life without her, and so this time the sobs were almost uncontrollable. Later, I lay there watching the shadows grow longer through the glass door.

"I can't see you anymore," Tanya began. "Cheri has become very upset. She knows what's been going on."

I stared as the crinkle at the side of her eye danced with playfulness. My sadness changed to anger. I snapped, "You're actually enjoying going with both of us!" I paused, shaking my head, then continued, "and leading me on!"

"No, Marilyn, I truly think a person can love more than one person at a time," Tanya said, a smile creeping across her thin lips.

My mind raced back to her words, *I love you,* that first night she'd made love to me. "So you *did* tell me that the first night," I said. "I had begun to doubt my own mind."

Tanya nodded, the crinkle at the corner of her eye still dancing.

"Yet now with one breath you're telling me you love me, and with the other, you're telling me goodbye!" I flopped back on the bed in despair.

"Cheri has given me an ultimatum. I must stop seeing you," she said as she brought her body over mine and gave me her goodbye kiss.

Only a few days later Tanya called and asked, "Can I see you again?" I felt as if I was on a roller coaster. This happened many times. She would see me, then she would tell me that she could not.

Tanya was playing us both, creating a triangle, but I wanted to stay blind to that fact. It had always been my policy never to become involved with a married man, but I didn't know what to do with this situation. I knew I didn't want to stop seeing her. It was as if she had unexplainable, intensifying control over me. I felt I was no longer in charge of my own fate, but that Tanya was in charge of it. I had reached a point of being totally and *insanely* in love with her. Then the small thought would enter my head of how much this was like the relationship with Madison, and that I was losing myself to Tanya, becoming powerless, the more I fell in love with her, just as I had with Madison.

My work began to suffer; I could rarely keep my mind on it. I began to hate *triangles.*

One day, as she'd done before, Tanya said, "I can't see you anymore." This time as I walked away I was determined that her words would finally be true and we would end this madness. I walked to my car, which was parked in front of the local coffee shop. Inside I had a large box filled with brochures that I was going to hand out that night at a charity. I felt my mind was about to snap from this last breakup, but as I leaned over to pick up the box it was something in my back that snapped. I stood there, unable to straighten up.

A woman affiliated with the charity ran over when she heard my yell. "Can I help? What's wrong?"

"My back, my back, I can't straighten up." I groaned in more pain than I could ever remember.

"I know a masseuse," the woman said. "I will drive you there." She led me to her car and we struggled to get my bent body through the door. I screamed in pain with each movement. When we arrived at the masseuse's we went through the same painful process to get me out of the car.

The masseuse looked at my back and asked, "What hit you?"

"Nothing hit me," I said, doubled over in pain, "I only bent over to lift something."

"I've never seen anything like this," she said in amazement. "You have a huge black and blue mark." She held a mirror at an angle so I could see what she was talking about.

I saw a large, black, oblong mark on the lower left side of my back. It was about four inches high and very narrow. It looked as if the end of a plank, a rifle butt, or something of that shape had hit me. She worked on my back as much as she could, but she couldn't do much as it was too sore.

"You won't be able to work for six weeks," the masseuse predicted. She was almost right—it was four.

When I first moved to the Islands, I'd set up a studio at the Hilton Hawaiian Village Hotel in Waikiki. It was the largest hotel in the world and people came there from all over.

After the fourth week of not being able to work, I knew I had to do *something*. I had portraits I needed to complete. The most pressing one was of a client who had recently moved to Paris. She wanted me to fly there for the final posing. It was going to be difficult to leave the Islands, it was going to be excruciatingly difficult to leave Tanya, but it wouldn't be difficult to leave her triangles. I knew I had to get on with my life.

I could finish all my other work, then go on to Paris, and perhaps I could continue on around the world. I ran the idea over and over in my mind. I considered traveling for a year. Maybe I'd *never* come back.

Tanya tried calling several times, but I'd just let the phone ring or have my answering machine record her message. She sensed that something had changed drastically. I could hear the desperation growing in her voice with each new message.

I was at my studio in the Hilton Hawaiian Village when one day she showed up unexpectedly.

"I just had to see you," she said, her pale green eyes trying to penetrate the wall I had thrown up between us. As I tried to avoid looking at her eyes in order to maintain a distance between us, she just kept coming closer and closer until she'd put her hand over mine. The surging passion once again went through my body and I nearly dropped the brush I was holding.

"You've been on my mind a lot. I've really missed you." I could hear a sense of urgency growing in her voice, yet she was almost purring.

"I've been busy," I started slowly. "I missed some work because of my back and now I'm trying to catch up."

"Let me buy you lunch," she said as she linked her arm in mine. Soon she was leading me around the corner to a small pizza parlor.

We ordered and sat in silence. When the waitress brought the pizza, I tore off a small piece and announced, "I have a portrait commission to finish in Paris, so I'll be leaving in a few days."

Tanya's eyes followed my hands as if mesmerized as I picked off a piece of pepperoni and guided it toward my mouth. I chewed it slowly before I went on. "I might continue on around the world. I think I need to get away for a while." And then, spontaneously, impulsively, as if driven by an inner date with destiny, I added, "Would you like to go with me?"

For a moment, I remembered how my Uncle Llewellyn had forced me to make a decision about Madison so many years ago in New York, and I decided to go for it all. "You have fifteen minutes to decide."

I saw her eyes widen in disbelief at my unusual "take charge" statement. I turned away so she couldn't see the pallor of fear cross my face and I took a bite of the thin-crusted pizza. I had just decided to gamble it all—I would now go to Paris, perhaps to leave her for good—or else she might say "Yes" and come with me. I knew if she said "Yes", she would leave Cheri and we would be together. I also had a pervasive feeling there would be no turning back from our destiny and that those green eyes that I knew from somewhere would have a transformative effect on my life.

I let the somber mantle of silence hang over us until I was sure fifteen minutes had passed and then I turned back to face her. Her pale green eyes looked squarely at me, piercing into me; perhaps they had been doing that the whole time. Where did I know those eyes from? Why did I feel my knees shaking? Why was I suddenly so afraid? *Why did I feel that this had happened to me before?*

"Yes, I want to go with you," her voice purred as I watched the green of her eyes darken as if a cloud had passed overhead.

Suddenly my strength, my power, and my confidence all drained from me. It was as if she had called me at my own game, as if she had taken back the controls and I was now committed to something I didn't know how to turn back from. I looked at her deep green eyes and murmured, "I'll arrange for your ticket."

Chapter Fifteen

The Mountain

Between the idea and the reality, Between the motion and the act . . . falls the Shadow:

—T. S. ELIOT
The Hollow Men

It had been a long time since I'd been to Paris. I didn't know how I'd feel about being there. So *much* had changed in my life. It was as if for the second time I'd be honeymooning there, but this time with a woman, and *again* without a license.

I booked a small, quaint hotel on the Left Bank. I've always wanted to live there. I thought, maybe someday I will.

One of the first things I did in Paris was call a salon and arrange for a new haircut, that free and abandoned look only a Parisian hair stylist can create. I caught my image reflecting back at me as I returned to the hotel and I liked what I saw.

My career was going well, I was embarking on a new relationship with Paris, which was my city, and I felt excited about sharing it all with Tanya. A new strength entered me. I knew I would be able to finish the portrait and that I would now be able to have new purpose and meaning in my life. I couldn't wait to go to one of the city's wonderful fountains and share its classical beauty with Tanya. I was sure the cascading, refreshing water would refresh my spirit as well.

As the taxi sped through the streets, I heard one of those pulsing sirens far off in the distance, and as if experiencing something from another time, I shuddered.

The taxi driver barely understood the address I'd given him. We drove up and down the streets while he shook his head. "No, no, can't be," he said. "There are a lot of mansions around here."

He stopped in front of what must have once been a palace. He was still shaking his head as I pointed to the address I had written on a piece of paper and pointed to the same number above the doorway. He reluctantly agreed he would wait for me while I went to check if it was the right place. I'd tried to call my client earlier, but could find no listing.

I stepped out of the cab and went up the long marble steps and entered the open doorway. I looked around the large entrance lobby for an intercom system since it looked like there might be different apartments in the building.

I walked to the right of the lobby and started up the wide and majestic circular steps. On the second floor I saw a doorway with brilliant purple surrounding it. I knew instantly I'd found my client's residence. I ran down the steps, retrieved my canvas and paints from the cab, and then walked back up to my client's very purple doorway and rang the bell.

I'd begun the portrait of Mrs. Tanaka in Honolulu. She was very fair, red-haired, and eccentric. She was married to one of the wealthiest men in the world. His family owned the world's largest hotel chain. Since she was not Japanese, his family did not approve of her. She had been raised as a diplomat's daughter and had traveled all over the world, and when she and Hiroshi met, he was fascinated by her recklessness and flamboyance and he had to have her. She held out and did not make love to him until he had married her. Now he had her ensconced in a mansion in Paris to keep her from his family's scrutiny.

As she ushered me in the door, I could see she was making the most of her exile. She had house painters everywhere. They were painting the entire apartment in brilliant purple enamel. She confirmed that the building had once been a palace and that it was now divided into two very large apartments.

There was hand-carved filigree everywhere, over the mantels, the windows, around the many pillars, and where the walls met the ceiling. It was clear this place had once been opulent. Now it was all turning a deep, royal purple, her favorite color. One day, when she moves out, I could hardly imagine what the owner of the apartment would think, trying to remove all this shiny purple enamel paint from everything, especially the hand-carved filigree.

There was almost no furniture. She said she'd selected it but it took forever to get it delivered, just as it did to get a phone installed in Paris, which was why I'd been unable to find a listing for her.

"You must see my dining room," she said as she led me across the marble floor of the living room. We walked into a large, dark room with no windows. It was painted entirely in black enamel. Everything in it was black except for the ceiling, which was completely covered by large, smoke-colored mirrors. Small twinkling lights glowed from under the glass of a twelve-foot-long, black dining table. A most unforgettable room . . . especially for anyone who ever dined there.

Mrs. Tanaka *was* a full-bloom eccentric. She nonchalantly told me Hiroshi had not sent her spending money yet so she was borrowing from the painters. Thank goodness she'd paid for the portrait and the European traveling expenses in advance.

I set up my easel and unrolled the canvas I'd brought from Honolulu, where we had the first posing. The portrait was nearly finished, showing her in a designer gown sitting elegantly on a sofa. I had her bare feet tucked slightly under the edge of her gown. I had arranged her that way thinking the contrast of the formal and the casual would suggest a *bit* of her eccentricity.

Sashi, as she wanted me to call her, was delighted with the look I had given her. She insisted that all of the men painting the apartment stop their work and come see her new portrait. She popped open some champagne and we all shared a toast to her.

The time with Sashi was wonderful and crazy, yet I was delighted when I could exit the purple mansion and head back to the hotel and Tanya. Several hours had passed and I was anxious to tell her about my "purple" experience.

"Marilyn," Tanya began before I could speak, "this will be my city. I've had such an exciting day."

"Wonderful, Tanya. The portrait is finished so we have all this time to explore *Gay Paree.*"

I was so glad that Tanya loved Paris, I had been worried about her. On the flight over she'd turned very silent. She hadn't told me she was afraid of flying, but I gave her a Dramamine when I saw her hands gripping the armrests of her seat. After that, she slept most of the time and when she wasn't sleeping she was very quiet. I didn't pay much attention to it all because I loved to fly so much. In fact, I'd always said one of my greatest fantasies would be to fly without a plane.

After we'd arrived in Paris? Tanya had seemed a little lost and I became concerned about whether she'd enjoy the trip at all. Still, I was determined that I would enjoy it since Paris was one of my first loves, so finding Tanya bubbling and excited about Paris delighted me.

"I've found this wonderful small cafe where we can dine tonight," she said with her old sense of command. "I've made all the arrangements."

That night as we talked over dinner, we decided that since my work was finished and we had two weeks to spend as we pleased that we would not only see Paris, but would also explore some of the rest of Europe. I would be able to show Tanya some of the castles and mountains I'd visited years before.

We caught a train to Switzerland, got off at Lucerne, and arranged for a hotel. Gigantic mountains surrounded us everywhere. I'd always had an affinity for mountains and was anxious to go to the top of one. A series of tram rides would take us up 15,000 feet to a glacier we could walk through.

The tram swayed back and forth on the cable as we started up to the first level, and my heart began to pound. I was thrilled with the feeling of flying, the beauty of the deep blue mountain, and the thought of going to the top of it. It was something I'd dreamed of doing my whole life.

I glanced over at Tanya. Her hands were wrapped tightly around the rail. They were taut and white and so was her face. I stepped closer to her and put my hand over one of hers. She did not look at me, she did not move.

Tanya said nothing as we exited the tram at the first stop. I began walking toward the next tram. Tanya did not. "Tanya, let's get to the next tram," I said as I turned back. I tried to take her hand.

She threw my hand aside. "No," she said emphatically. "I don't want to ride any more trams." She was still white and now she was shaking as well.

"Okay, I'll just go on to the top and meet you back down here," I said. "You can rest and enjoy a cup of coffee." I had noticed there was a restaurant on that level and motioned toward it.

Though Tanya was still white, she had nodded to me, and because of that and since this was something I'd always wanted to do, I decided to go on to the top alone.

I looked over and saw that all the other people who had ridden to the first level with us were already aboard the next tram, and I raced to join them.

As I jumped aboard, I felt like I was flying. The wind blew through my hair, the cool breeze brushed by my cheek, and my heart started pounding wildly. I felt such freedom that I thought it would only be greater if I were to sprout wings and fly to the top of the mountain.

The glacier was blue-white inside. It had a tunnel through it that was tall enough so that I could walk upright. The walkway was not that cold though its translucent walls were made of pure ice. Brilliant white light from the sun filtered down through the walls and surrounded me with a radiance that seemed angelic. I felt so alive!

An hour later I returned to where I had left Tanya. She looked absolutely traumatized. Her makeup was smeared down her cheeks and her eyes were red. As if I'd been hit by a blow to my stomach, my feeling of exhilaration vanished. I put my arms around her, thinking some deep tragedy must have happened. She pushed me away and snarled, "You left me. You took the passports and all the money and you left me."

From then on, all logic or reasoning was gone. She scolded, battered, and yelled at me as we descended the rest of the mountain and caught the train into Lucerne. Once there, as we walked toward our hotel, me often shuffling behind, I felt like the streets were closing in around me like the bars of a prison cell. Tanya kept bashing me with words: "You are thoughtless. You are heartless. You are cruel. You *abandoned* me."

Any words I tried to say were cut off by her words, words that were like knives through my heart. I finally collapsed on a curb and sobbed. How could this be happening with a woman I loved so much?

A figure in a dark uniform loomed above me. I stopped sobbing for a moment as the last rays of the day's sunlight caught a reflection from his badge. I knew he was wondering, just like I was, if my sanity was slipping.

"No, I'm all right," I said. "Yes, I'll get up. I'm only a short way from my hotel." Tanya had walked on and watched from across the street. When I turned, she was gone. I walked back to the hotel alone.

Once back in the hotel room, her barrage started again, only this time she hit me with her angry fists in cadence with her angry words. In my life, I'd never fought back and I didn't now. I only put up my arms as shields against the blows. One blow caught me hard, knocking me backward. I felt a sharp pain at the back of my head, then blackness engulfed me.

Only moments later I came to and Tanya was standing over me. She looked as shocked as I was. I felt totally defeated. I got up and walked silently to the bed on the far side of the room, next to a window, and I crawled under the covers, shaking.

I heard Tanya walk to the other bed. It was dark now. I looked out the window at the millions of stars above. I felt so small and lost as I watched a star fall from the sky and disappear.

For a long time, I just lay there thinking. My mind jumped between despair and desperation: despair over another violent relationship and desperation over the fear of losing her. I would think that surely we can't go on and then I'd wonder, was this how my new relationship was supposed to end? Done in by a mountain? Maybe we should just catch the train back to Paris and then each go our own separate ways. I would give her her ticket and she could do whatever she wanted. She'd looked so fragile—like a little girl—and I felt so guilty for having left her on that mountain.

Then from somewhere deep inside me, a memory started surfacing—a memory of a child, a small child with pale green eyes. The memory hovered before me like a vague, fluid mist that I could not fully grasp, and I began to repeat: *maybe I'm supposed to protect her, maybe I should never have left her there by the side of*—was it a mountain?—Strange, but I kept seeing the side of a ditch, *the side of a ditch in a forest.* Yet it was a forest I knew I never had been to. My mind reeled dizzily—maybe we have met for a reason—maybe I should *never leave her.* My obsession with her had become so deep, I then fell into the bone-chilling, icy fear *that she would leave me.*

I lay awake for hours, staring at the stars. In the middle of the night, Tanya rose from her bed and came over to mine. She lifted the covers and crawled in next to me, then curled up like a kitten and fell asleep. I lay awake for hours, stunned, dazed, and confused, wondering about her bizarre behavior and about the vision I'd just had of Tanya by a ditch in a forest, a forest we'd never been to.

When I awoke the next morning, she was already up and packing. I felt panic as I pictured her walking out the door and out of my life. Now I knew I was desperately in love with her and that I needed her. I also felt that we had met for a reason, even though I wasn't aware of what that reason was.

My eyes followed her as she walked back and forth, carrying clothes to her suitcase. Maybe I should let her go. How could I be in love with someone who knocked me out the night before? My thoughts kept pummeling at my sanity, as did the recurring vision of the ditch and the forest. Then I realized she was also packing my bags.

"Let's go get some breakfast and get on with seeing Europe," she said as if nothing had happened.

We never again spoke of the events of the previous day and I never climbed any more mountains.

The rest of the trip was a dizzying whirlwind. I never was able to find the castle I'd been to as a student—with the feather comforter and the portrait in the hall. I'd wanted to show Tanya the portrait I'd seen so long ago of the Queen with the pale green eyes and the pink, triangled bodice. I wanted to show her how much it looked like her.

Most of the time we traveled in silence. Tanya often seemed fragile and lost, and that just made me want to protect her even more. Perhaps she looked so vulnerable because we were in places that were not familiar to her. I was sure everything would be okay when we went home to *start our new life together.*

As the days went by, I got caught more and more in the web of needing her and as I did the fear kept growing that she would leave me unless I did everything I could think of to please her. From somewhere I'd connected powerlessness with love and thought you were never supposed to say "no" to someone you loved.

After our two weeks we boarded the plane to go back to the United States. I watched her knuckles turn white as she gripped the armrests and the plane rose into the sky. She never spoke to me during the entire flight back and I wondered if I'd done something wrong or if it was just that she feared flying as much as she feared riding a tram.

I knew her fear was because she had no control over planes or trams.

Chapter Sixteen

The Pool

Every tear from every eye
Becomes a babe in eternity

> —WILLIAM BLAKE
> *Poems from the Pickering Manuscript*

Tanya moved into my Niu Valley home when we returned from Europe. One of the first things she insisted on was the removal of my waterbed. "I don't like waterbeds," she said flatly.

After a few days I called Leilani. Her son answered the phone. "She's not well at all—maybe you should come see her."

Leilani was already standing at the door as I drove up her steep drive. She took my hand. "I need to talk to you," she said. "But not in this house."

I drove the car back down the steep hill and swung out onto the highway along the ocean. We rode in silence for a while, then I turned out to the sea wall near the lighthouse and stopped the car. We sat watching the waves. I was hoping that some of the sadness of the trip would wash out with the tide and that the white-capped waves would bring in fresh hope and happiness for my relationship with Tanya.

I looked over at Leilani. Her hands were clenched tightly together. "Leilani, why don't you tell me what's going on with you?"

I saw a tear forming at the corner of her eye. Like a frightening omen, the hairs began to rise on the back of my neck even before she began her story.

One day, a couple of weeks ago, she left her real estate office and drove home around midday.

"This was really a rare thing for me to do, but something was bothering me," she said. "Something told me I just needed to check the house. I walked through the house looking for Misty—you know, my little white poodle. I couldn't find her anywhere in the house and so I turned to go out the door to the deck. The door was ajar, so I dashed through it and out on to the deck by the pool."

Leilani's words began to come faster. "I saw Misty struggling and paddling in the pool. Her eyes were huge with fear." Leilani's words began racing over one another and she shook her head from side to side as if reenacting her panic. "When I reached down to pull Misty out, it was as if something pushed me from behind, as if a force pushed me, and I fell into the pool. I kept trying to reach the sides, but they were slippery and I just kept sliding back down into the pool."

Leilani's pool was one of those types with a blue liner held above the ground by braces. There are no steps leading out of the pool, only a hand rail to grab to pull yourself out.

"Every time I got near the side of the pool, it felt like something was pushing me away and I kept getting more and more frightened." Her tears began to spill over. "Poor Misty was getting so tired. I tried to lift her up from the water to put her on the deck, but I couldn't get near it. Something kept pushing me back. Once I was able to grab the bars leading out, but they felt so hot I couldn't hang on." Leilani's eyes got wider. "Even when the sun was the hottest, I don't remember that ever happening before.

"The few times I got near the side of the pool and tried to grab the deck, I lost my grip and just slid back down the blue siding." The tears were darkly staining her golden cheeks.

"Marilyn, I struggled that way for hours. The only thing that saved me was I remembered my swimming lessons and started floating, first on my back, then on my face. I was so exhausted, I didn't think I could go on." Leilani was wringing her hands together, folding first the right over the left and then the left over the right. "I knew I was on my last breath just as Eric came running through the door yelling for me."

Eric, Leilani's eighteen-year-old son, was a weight lifter.

"Thank God for Eric—thank God. I was slipping under when he grabbed my hair and pulled me to the side of the pool." Leilani's lashes brushed her cheek and smeared away the tears that stung her flesh with salt.

"Whatever force had kept me away from the side of the pool earlier was gone and Eric was able to drag me up on the deck. I just lay there exhausted," she said, shaking her head from side to side, ". . . I just lay there . . . exhausted and drained!" She paused a long while before she went on.

"Eric dove in and pulled Misty from the bottom of the pool." Tears burst over her lids and glistened against her skin. "When I saw him lay her poor, limp little body on the deck, I couldn't help it, Marilyn. I was so *hurt* and *angry,* I screamed at them, 'YOU DAMN NIGHT STALKERS—YOU DAMN GHOSTS—YOU DAMN MURDERERS!'"

Leilani was now sobbing. "I'm so afraid. I know I shouldn't have cursed them, but they killed Misty—they *nearly* killed me."

I reached for her and folded my arms around her shaking, sobbing body, "Marilyn," she cried, "I don't know what to do."

I held her and cradled her for a long time. I didn't know what to do, either. I couldn't give her many reassuring words, I was also afraid, afraid for *her.* After Leilani had told me the second time about seeing the Night Stalkers, I'd talked to a Hawaiian Kahuna priest about her case.

"The Night Stalkers are sacred warriors, here to protect the Hawaiian lands," the Kahuna had said, confirming what I'd heard before. "They exist in another time and dimension. You could say that we walk in the same places, but we can't see them. They co-exist peacefully with those of us who live in the third dimension."

"Do they ever come into our dimension? Does anyone ever see them?" I asked.

"They only come forth and are seen when they feel there's a threat."

I told him about Leilani seeing the Night Stalkers. "But," I protested, "Leilani never threatened them. I'm convinced it was the previous owners of the house, the people who were into black magic, who threatened them and the land."

"Yes," the Kahuna agreed. "It's possible that it was the previous owners who drew the Night Stalkers into our third dimension. And now they're staying around to make sure all is well. *Perhaps if she never threatens them* . . ." His voice drifted off for a moment.

"This is all very unusual." He rolled his eyes and added, "Usually when someone has seen the Night Stalkers, there's nothing you can do!"

Now I was very frightened for Leilani. I knew she had seen the Night Stalkers and that *now* she had cursed them . . . *now she had threatened them!*

* * *

Several days later Leilani came to see me. She appeared much calmer and thanked me for listening to her story.

"I guess the hardest part is how much I miss Misty," she said.

I wanted to get her to talk more about her sadness, but she promptly changed the subject and asked me about my trip to Europe. I told her about Mrs. Tanaka and her "purple palace" apartment. I avoided telling her about Tanya's violent outburst or the pain of the long silences between us.

It had been clear to me for some time that Leilani did not like Tanya. Leilani then asked how my personal life was going, my home life.

"You know you're losing a lot of your friends, Marilyn. And, no, it's not your lifestyle." She laughed for the first time that day, then winked and said, "You know that old saying, 'Some of my best friends are gay.' No, your lifestyle doesn't bother me, but what's happening to you bothers me. You don't laugh much anymore."

"Yes, that's probably true," I agreed, turning my eyes away from her gaze, and not wanting to think about that or about how much I hurt inside.

Leilani sensed my hurt. Not sure of its cause, but sensitive to it, she switched the subject to reincarnation.

"You know, Marilyn, I think it's possible we've all lived before and have all loved differently. Maybe I've loved a woman in another lifetime." She fixed her eyes firmly on me as she went on. "There's got to be more than just this life. How could we accomplish everything we need to in just one lifetime?"

"Yes, Leilani, I'm beginning to think that's exactly what's happened to me. I had a bleed-through into another life."

I told her more about the rough stone wall and the leather boots that sometimes appear in those strange episodes. And about how I'd often become disoriented and my hands would change into a man's.

"Leilani, I'm beginning to think we meet the people we're supposed to meet and that we get involved with them for a reason. That could be the explanation for love at first sight, that we are attracted to people we've known before, in other lifetimes. Of course, once we've found each other, we discover that we have something that we must work out together. I've got to believe this," I added, pausing, "or I'd think I was going crazy."

"For sure, I've met Tanya for a reason." I studied Leilani's face for the approval that didn't come. "I'd been floating aimlessly for years before meeting her. That's why she's good for me—she grounds me."

"Yes," Leilani replied, "and some people like to pull the wings off butterflies."

We sat in silence for a long while. Finally I said, "Approve or not, I'd like you to help us find a house, something unusual."

"What's wrong with the one you have?"

"Well, it bothers Tanya that it was originally mine."

Leilani only shook her head, and stared at my lowered head. "I'll look," said after a long while.

Another Interlude

The life which is unexamined is not worth living.
—PLATO
Dialogues, Phaedrus

The first hint of sunrise appeared across the Sedona sky, and I lay on my feather comforter watching the scarlet rays spread across the horizon. The lower left side of my back throbbed. Apollo nudged my arm. "Hey, stalker, you'll have to wait to go out." I pushed the hair back from his eyes and scratched his little head.

I had been writing for weeks now, pouring out the events of my life from so many years ago. For a while, it seemed that each day I had grown lighter. One day when I left my house and my reclusiveness, a friend stopped me on the street. "You look ten, fifteen years younger," she said in amazement. "What have you been doing?"

I threw my head back and said with a laugh, "I've been throwing up a lot," then added almost as an afterthought, "getting rid of poisons I've swallowed through the years."

I had written about the pathos, the tragedy, and the fear of my life with Madison, reliving every moment as I put it down on the page. Could all of this really have happened, I wondered, and yet I knew it had. I felt I had dealt with everything that had happened with Madison except perhaps the "why's": *Why* I had chosen some-one who was so abusive and controlling; *Why* I had made myself so powerless.

The issue loomed before me again, as I knew I must deal with my powerlessness with Tanya. I knew this was going to be even more difficult to write about. It wasn't so far removed in time so I wasn't sure if I'd finished handling it emotionally as I had regarding Madison. I also knew I had to continue connecting the pieces, the maze of all the déjà vu experiences with their unexplained and disori-enting other-world memories, so I could further discover the destruc-tive patterns that had controlled so much of my life. As I thought about all this, the pain in my back increased.

Shortly after moving to Sedona, I had remodeled my house. I had taken out the back wall of the bedroom and replaced it with sliding glass doors so I could feel like I was outdoors. This gave me a wonderful feeling of freedom. Now as I lay there looking out, I caught the pink of the sunrise along the horizon and watched it deepen.

My backache had begun several days ago, starting in the lower left side and getting more severe each day. At times my leg went numb, but mostly I felt a deep throbbing in my back.

I knew what the connection was: besides getting close in my writings to the time of my desperate search for reincarnational pat-terns, I would be exploring the black-and-blue mark that had mysteri-ously appeared on my back's lower left side shortly after I had met Tanya.

Also I knew it was time to go emotionally deeper into the amputation of what was left. I thought back to my dream of only a few weeks ago—the dream of having my left leg amputated. First, in the dream, I had removed dry husks—they had symbolized removing the empty shells of hurt that had remained from my relationship with Madison. Now, as in the dream, I was about to go deeper into the leg and find the live, festering seed pods, and I knew they would symbolize dealing with the anguish that remained of my relationship with Tanya. Yes, I was about to ampu-tate my left leg—"amputate" what was *"left!"* Perhaps then I could finish learning what I needed to know about past patterns and the connective link between lifetimes.

Apollo's nudging had become more urgent. "All right, all right," I said, scratching his little black head again, "I'll take you for your walk now." I rose, put on my clothes, attached his lead to his collar, and grabbed my Dictaphone as I went out the door. Who knows, I might meet another rabbit, one that could interpret my dreams for me, or perhaps clarify the next part of my story—a part that's more like a nightmare.

Chapter Seventeen

A Castle Not To Be

A huge gap appeared in the side of the
Mountain ... At last a tiny mouse came forth.
                                        —AESOP
                              The Mountain in Labor

Every Sunday it became a ritual for Tanya and me to go house-hunting. Like so many other things in our relationship, looking for a house came with a sense of urgency, as if finding the right house might make everything okay between us. This pervasive urgency always directed our relationship; rarely was there peacefulness.

As I had slipped deeper and more desperately in love with her, I felt like a drowning person clinging to the side of a sinking ship. I had also slipped more fully into the role of her protector, though I'm not sure I had any sense of what I was really protecting her *from*. I only knew that I had to protect this person, who I thought was so fragile, from her feelings, all the while burying my own feelings as my head was slipping further and further under the water.

Tanya and I both clung to the relationship as if it was our life raft.

Sometimes on the way home from my studio at the Hilton Hawaiian Village, I would stop by the ocean and watch the waves for what seemed like an eternity, trying to figure out why our lives had come together and what my part was.

Perhaps what Leilani and I had discussed was true: you meet the people you're supposed to meet so you can work out your karma. Then, I would spend hours trying to figure out what our karma was—why I was with her and why the green eyes gripped me so. I thought back to the portrait I had seen in the castle so many years earlier during my first trip to Europe. As time had passed, I realized more and more that there was a resemblance between Tanya and the Queen. I was so sorry I hadn't been able to find that portrait again when Tanya and I had recently gone to Europe so I could show her how much she looked like the Queen.

Leilani had found quite a few houses for us to look at. She was particularly excited about the one she was showing us today.

To enter it, you had to cross over a bridge that stretched over a stream that looked like a moat. The house had been built on a steep hillside, with large pillars stretching down from its base and into the rocks below. Floor-to-ceiling windows covered the entire curved living room and gave an unimpeded view of Honolulu and the ocean. On each side of the room, circular staircases led up to round rooms that resembled turrets.

"The architect designed this house for himself and his family," Leilani said. Her brown eyes danced and reflected how pleased she was that she'd found such an unusual home to show us. "He's thought of everything and spared no expense."

Tanya dashed on ahead. I could tell she was very excited about it.

As I crossed over the moat, my eyes began to water. A warm liquid seemed to form around them and I became dizzy. I reached the door to the circular living room, but had to grab the rail of the stairs that led down into that room so I wouldn't fall. I looked around desperately for a place to sit down.

At the base of the windows was a built-in sofa, so I eased myself onto it and faced away from the windows. I could not look out. I could not look down.

My breath was coming hard, my heart was racing. I felt the warm liquid still gathering around my eyes. Then suddenly the windows were replaced by rough stone walls with flickering torches lining them. *Oh God—not here—please, not here, please, not again!* My eyes blurred as I slipped into another time.

I saw a young woman with pale green eyes and a pink velvet bodice walking toward me, adjusting the crown that sat on her soft brown hair.

I quickly closed my eyes, not wanting to believe what I was seeing. I squeezed my lids tightly together and tried to remove all visual sensation as I flopped back against the sofa. Instantly the warm liquid receded, as did the rough stones and the flickering torches and the young woman with the crown.

Tanya came racing toward me, her eyes flashing. "Take my hand," she said. "We'll climb the turret together."

I rose slowly, weakly, from the sofa. Tanya was so excited that she didn't even notice how my hand was trembling. We walked to the stairway at the left that led to the second floor. She wrapped her fingers tightly around mine as she led me up the circular stairway. My knees were still weak, so with my other hand, I clasped the rail along the wall.

We came into the sunlight at the top of the stairs. Tanya guided me across the room. As she pulled me closer to the round windows, I thought back to the turrets in the castle in Germany so many years ago and how that was the first time I'd ever been afraid of heights.

"Look at my world—look at *our* world," she said, squeezing my hand sharply and pinching my fingers against my ring so hard that I gasped.

We were standing on a mountain above Honolulu, the whole city spread out before us. Beyond the city, we could see the deep, azure blue of the ocean. Immediately beneath us was a densely wooded area where I could picture small creatures running, playing, and hiding in the underbrush.

Tanya turned to me and pulled her hand slowly across my cheek before she pressed her lips softly, sensuously against mine. My knees grew unsteady again as I looked into her pale green eyes, the pale eyes that resembled the haunting green eyes of the Queen in the castle portrait I'd seen long ago.

Tanya pulled at my arm and I returned from my thoughts. We walked back down the stairway and again entered the living room.

"This is it—this is our castle! I must have it!" Tanya's voice was breaking with excitement.

Castle. Had she used the word "castle?" Maybe that's it—maybe we had shared a life together in a castle. Then why was I trembling so and what was I afraid of?

As Leilani drove us down the hill, Tanya continued a non-stop monologue about the house and how we could arrange everything from financing to furniture. I mostly stayed silent. All the while,

Leilani kept looking from Tanya to me. Whether she approved of Tanya or not, I knew she had come to accept us as a couple.

Tanya noticed my silence for the first time when we reached the bottom of the hill. "What's the matter, Marilyn? Don't you love the house, too?"

"Yes," I replied slowly, "I loved the view and I did think the house was beautiful and unusual." I formed the words slowly; I didn't want to provoke any anger from Tanya, which I knew my disjointed, karmic thoughts would do. "But I think I would have to see it again. I got a little dizzy from the heights."

I could see Tanya's eyes flash with rage. Her voice raised a pitch as her words pelted me. "You *know* I love that house! You *know* I want it!" Then as quickly as the anger rose, her purring came. "Think of all the fun we can have making it ours, all the wonderful evenings we'll have together."

I dropped my head and my voice and I murmured, "We'll go see it again."

We went back to see the house several times. After the third visit, Leilani called me at my studio. "Marilyn, what is going on?"

"I don't know, Leilani. Something happens to me when I go into that house. Remember those incidents I told you about long ago with my eyes floating in liquid and how dizzy and disoriented I would become? Well it happens to me every time I enter that house. It's so much like an old castle. I don't think I can handle it, but I don't know how to tell Tanya. She wants it so much."

Leilani's pause was long and deliberate. She was waiting for me to find the courage to say *no* to purchasing the house. When she could no longer stand the wait or the pain she knew I was feeling, she said, "I could tell Tanya the house has already been sold."

"Thanks, Leilani, but I couldn't live with that kind of a lie," I said. "I will have to tell her that I just can't stand the height."

"You can go to the top of a mountain, but you can't live on a hill," Tanya yelled at me. "That's pitiful."

Tanya was furious. It was the first time I had ever said *no* to her.

A couple of days later, Leilani and I met for lunch. It was clear to Leilani that my distress was now matching hers.

"Marilyn," Leilani began, "I've found a psychic who is really sensitive. I go to her regularly about my house, the haunting." She rolled her eyes as she went on. "Sometimes, I think it helps." She paused, adding, "Maybe she can help you find some answers about your volatile relationship."

Tears welled in the corners of my eyes. "I didn't know it showed that much."

I usually listened to Leilani's advice, but a psychic? Well, I just didn't know.

After a few days I called and made an appointment with the psychic Leilani had recommended. I was very apprehensive as I approached the door to her office. Please don't let her use tea leaves or a crystal ball, I said to myself. She didn't—she used Tarot cards.

She spread them out in front of her. "The Queen of Hearts—you have a woman in your life. You've known her before in another lifetime. She wasn't good for you then, and she's not good for you now.

"The Death card—I see death around you." She saw my face go white. She went on, "Now the Death card doesn't always mean physical death. It can mean a severe change, a deep change in your life—I think it's your relationship," She paused to see if I was getting some color back in my face. "Yes, the relationship you're in is smothering you. You need to think about making a change."

I glared at the reader in front of me. How dare she tell me I needed to change my relationship! She had no idea how desperately I loved Tanya. This was the person I was going to spend my life with. It was more than a relationship, it was *fated*. It had been written in the stars—it was *forever*.

I let her finish her reading, then I got up and walked out. I was all the more determined to make my relationship work. Tanya and I were supposed to be together, we had a *karmic reason* to be together. Tanya was my soul mate. I was *sure* that's why I'd fallen in love with her.

"Soul mates can work things out together." I knew that. That's also when the hardest lessons come up. With soul mates, there's an opportunity to work out all of the grist of one's life.

Ya, grist, I thought, *falling in love with a woman!* And that's why Tanya and I have all this pathos, that's why we're constantly on the edge of a crisis: we're burning away the chaff of our lives and our karma.

Since we weren't going to share our lives in the house with the turrets, *the castle* hanging from the hillside, we started searching even more desperately for a place to call home.

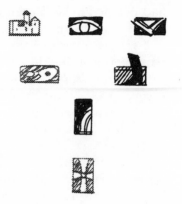

Chapter Eighteen

The Portrait

*The more unexplainable and mysterious it is, the more insight
it will yield when eventually explained.*
> —J. B. RHINE
> *The Reach of the Mind*

Tanya and I had been invited to a party at a large house by the
ocean. As we were mingling amongst the blend of people that was
so common in Hawaii—Chinese, Japanese, Hawaiian, and many
who were a composite of them all—I was sure we were the token
Caucasians and the token gay couple.

As usually happened at such functions, Tanya and I went our
separate ways. I glanced over and saw that she had found a large
high-backed chair that looked like a throne and was seated in it. She
had on a pink blouse that was buttoned right beneath her throat.
She looked beautiful, and I knew I must paint her, that this would
be the setting. I would use the high-backed chair and she would
wear her pink blouse with the lapel that formed a triangle.

Tanya sat with her legs slightly crossed and her arms at her sides
on the arm rests. One hand was draped lightly over the front of the
arm rest, and the sunlight sparkled off the large emerald-cut diamond
ring I had given her. I had traded a portrait for the ring. At first I

had planned to keep it for myself, but when Tanya had fallen in love with it, I ended up giving it to her.

I walked over to Tanya. "Darling, I want to paint you. I want to paint you just like this."

"Oh, wonderful—I'd love to pose for you," she said, her pale green eyes flashing with an unusual brilliance.

The hostess was genuinely pleased when I asked if we could use her setting for a portrait posing and we agreed to a time two days from then.

When we returned two days later, the hostess had the throne-chair waiting for us. Tanya struck a pose like a queen as I draped her skirt gracefully around her.

It's very difficult to paint someone you love. You can never do enough for them, and I wanted to please Tanya so much.

I knew I wouldn't need Tanya to pose very often—I could almost paint her from memory. I already had the vision of how the portrait should look. I would only have to take photos of her, retire to my studio, paint until it was nearly completed, and then have her sit for a final posing.

My vision of her portrait was clearly what I had seen that day in the house by the ocean: Tanya sitting regally in her pink blouse as if she were a queen.

I was in my studio working on her painting when my eyes began to water again. It had been some time since I'd felt my eyes floating in the warm liquid, but soon a total blur engulfed me . . .

"Take my hand—we're going to climb to the turret together," a voice said.

I tried desperately to clear my head, but I looked down and saw that I was wearing leather boots. And, I was wearing a soft deerskin tunic. I had a small dab of pink paint across the forefinger of my left hand. My hands were large and strong, and they were those of a man. As I slipped deeper into another time and place, my last thoughts were, *Oh my God, it's happening again: I'm a man.*

"Come, come, I want to show you the turret," a young woman with pale green eyes said to me as she adjusted the crown on her soft brown hair.

She grabbed my hand and clutched it tightly as she led me down the rough stone hallway. Her laugh was like that of a child on an outing and contrasted greatly with how she looked in the elegant satin gown.

We passed several blazing torches attached to the walls by heavy wrought iron scones. The flames from the torches cast eerie shadows across the walls and left a darkness in the crevices where the stone blocks met. By the flickering light I could see the olive-green of her eyes and the pink velvet of her triangular bodice.

Then she led me to an arched doorway where a circular flight of stairs led to the top of the turret.

She clutched my hand even more tightly as we came into the sunlight at the top of the stairs. She pulled me toward the edge of the turret. "I want you to see my world. Look at my world," she said as we stood right at the edge.

I looked out at the breathtaking expanse, and felt the hair rise at the back of my neck. Directly beneath us I saw a heavily wooded area teeming with deer and game. The animals would be hunted to feed everyone at the castle.

The Queen squeezed my fingers so tightly that I felt pain as my gold coin ring bit into my flesh. With her other hand, she reached up and gently stroked my beard before pressing her lips sensuously against mine.

"I have something else for you," she said as she flirtatiously led me back down the hall and through an open doorway. As we entered the room, we nearly bumped into an easel. It held a canvas. I looked over at it. It was a painting of . . . *her*. Pale green eyes stared out at me over a pink velvet bodice that formed a triangle and pointed downward from under her chin. Her soft brown hair was arranged just so around her face.

I looked down to see a dab of the same pink-colored paint on my forefinger. Just past the portrait, I could see a shadowy mirror hanging on a far wall. I caught a glimpse of the Queen and then myself in its silver murkiness. My dark hair was curled into loose ringlets that fell over my forehead, then met with a neatly trimmed yet full beard that stretched down to cover my lower face. I wore a soft, tan deerskin tunic over my broad shoulders and it blended perfectly with my hair and skin.

The Queen's tug at my hand drew me back from the mirror's shadow-world reflection and she pulled me past the portrait so quickly that we nearly tripped over the high-backed chair near it. Over in the corner I saw a bed with four high posters holding a soft golden canopy.

My mind was racing, my passions were racing. I knew the stirring in my body was not safe for an artist to have for a Queen, but I could no longer control them. She led me toward the bed and placed my hand against her breast as we lay down on the satin comforter.

The feathers rose up and consumed us as my passion consumed me.

I sat in my Honolulu studio, looking at my portrait of Tanya with its high-buttoned pink blouse. I sat a long time. My mind was a blur. It was already growing dark outside. I looked down at a small dab of pink paint on my delicate female hands that just moments before were a man's. My eyes looked back at Tanya's portrait and then past it to the large mirror that hung in shadow against a far wall. For a moment I thought I saw the Queen's portrait and the reflection of a young, bearded, dark-haired man standing before it. Then the blur cleared and I saw my blond hair and my bewildered smoke-blue eyes staring back at me. I was a woman again.

Tanya's pale green eyes gazed at me from the portrait I was painting. The same green eyes I'd moments before seen in the portrait of the Queen. Finally and totally, I realized that they were also the same pale green eyes I'd seen in the European castle so many years ago when I was visiting as a student.

I was dazed and frightened. I couldn't stop my hands from shaking. My mind was whirling, going over and over everything that had just happened. Was I going insane? Was I living two lives?

After a long, long while, when the sun had passed beneath the windowsill, I rose to head toward home.

Parts of this reality-shattering mystery were becoming clear to me now, though that didn't make it any less frightening. At least I knew it wasn't a dream, and I knew it wasn't a vision—it was too *real*. Finally, I accepted it all: I had lived *before*, I had been a *man*, an artist in the Queen's court, and I had been her lover.

Now that I knew all this, how was I going to live with it? What was I go to do with it? Should I tell Tanya? I knew, finally, who Tanya was and why her pale green eyes had always looked so familiar. I had painted her then and I was painting her now. It was all happening again, and now I knew. *Tanya was the Queen.*

*C*hapter Nineteen

With the Queen

The subconscious is not limited by our imposed boundaries of logic,
space. and time. It can remember everything, from any time.
                    —BRIAN L. WEIS, M.D.
                        Through Time Into Healing

Tanya found us a home on a hillside. It was much more expensive than the other one, but I knew I could not say *no* to her again.

Leilani understood that Tanya had to find the house for us herself. Though it was never discussed, she knew that Tanya no longer trusted her.

I decided not to tell Tanya about the past life flashback I'd had while I was doing her portrait. She wouldn't have believed me and would probably have gotten jealous. Wouldn't that be ironic, her getting jealous of herself in another lifetime that she doesn't even believe in.

The flashbacks to my life in the castle were becoming more frequent. I never knew for sure if or when they were going to occur, but they always came when I was working on Tanya's portrait. At first, they were frightening and disturbing, and I wondered if I was beginning to lose my mind. I also was afraid that I might flash to my life with the Queen and not be able to return to this one, and to Tanya. But I always returned.

Each time the flashbacks occurred, my eyes blurred, the warm liquid formed around them, and then I'd find myself standing at the easel in front of the Queen's portrait with her seated in front of me, flirting with me while I painted.

But I was soon to learn that the time sequences in regressive flashbacks to another lifetime do not always follow chronologically.

On one occasion, as I saw my hand change from female to male, I found myself being led down the torch-lit castle walkway for what I knew was the first time. I'd just been selected—in fact, had been *ordered*—to paint the Queen's portrait. Arrangements had been made for me to send my equipment on ahead. Servants ushered me into a large room where my easel and paints were waiting for me.

I had told them I would need a room with plenty of northern light. I now stood in the room that had been chosen. A large high-backed chair sat only a few feet in front of my easel. I looked around the room and saw a small table with two hand-carved chairs. Over in a far corner I saw the bed with high posters that held its golden canopy. A large, satin comforter was spread over the bed.

I stood in front of the easel and arranged my paints as I waited for the Queen.

She entered, followed by two servants who carried her train. She approached the high-backed chair and seated herself in a regal manner, wearing a gown that practically consumed her. Her pink velvet bodice formed a triangle that pointed downward from her chin. Her soft brown hair was arranged very carefully around her face. She looked at me intensely with her pale green eyes, then lifted her hands, clapped them softly together, and said, "Begin."

I knew this flashback was our first meeting.

As Tanya's portrait developed, so did the Queen's. With each flashback, the portrait deepened and so did the desire I felt for the Queen. One particular day as her prismatic green eyes stared back at me, I wondered, "Can she see the fire that burns throughout my body? Can she tell that I desire her?"

It was clear I was afraid to let the Queen know of my feelings. A theme of powerlessness was being exposed to me as I went deeper into the lifetime with the Queen, a theme that strangely matched how I felt with Tanya, and had begun to eat into my entire being.

But on this day as the Queen looked at me and said, "Take my hand, we're going to the turret together," I set all caution aside and raced recklessly down the hall with her.

In each flashback, she dismissed the servants as our portrait sessions began. It wasn't long before she suggested that I move into the castle. I was beginning to enjoy my time with her so much that

I sometimes didn't want to return to my life with Tanya, yet I always did. I felt she needed me.

I grew to know that the Queen had many lovers, but I also knew that I was her favorite. Each day as we met, I fell more in love with her and each day it became exceedingly more painful to think of her with others.

Then one day, Tanya's portrait was nearly complete and so was the Queen's. I had begun to paint a cold, severe expression on the Queen's portrait and I knew it was happening because of my jealousy over sharing her with other lovers. I also knew that with these feelings, I would continue to paint her expression with increased coldness. To keep that from happening, I had to finish the portrait that day. Then, there was something else I had to do—I had to say goodbye to the Queen.

I signed the painting and approached the Queen as she was sitting in her regal chair. I clasped one of her delicate young hands as I fell on my knees in front of her.

"Your highness," I said as I looked into her pale green eyes. Before I could go on, she reached down with her other hand and playfully stroked the left side of my face, tugging gently at the hairs of my beard.

"Your Highness, your royal portrait is finished." I reached up and placed my hand over hers as she tugged even more forcefully at my beard, and went on, "I love you desperately, but I must leave the castle now."

She pulled one hand from mine and the other from my beard, yanking out several hairs with her gesture. She said nothing, but I saw her colorless green eyes turn to ice.

After a long silence, I rose from my kneeling position and bowed. I continued bowing as I backed from the room. I didn't know what else to do. She only narrowed her lids around her ice-green eyes.

Out in the hall, I retraced my steps, going past the rough stone walls and torches I'd first seen when I'd entered the castle so many months before. I passed the archway that led onto the turret that the Queen and I had climbed so many times together. I decided to take one last look at the forest I loved so much and I climbed the steps, then walked out onto the turret. I went to the edge and looked out over the majestic landscape. "Yes," I thought, "this is the Queen's world, but it is not mine."

Chapter Twenty

The Confession

Nothing can bring you peace but yourself.
—RALPH WALDO EMERSON
Self Reliance

The phone rang, waking me up. I looked at the clock: 5:00 A.M. Why would anyone be calling at that hour? It was my sister-in-law, Grace, calling from Minnesota.

"Sorry to call you so early, but your mom's not well—she's been asking for you."

"What's wrong?" I asked, rubbing my eyes and trying to wake up.

"Well, it's hard to say. It's not life-threatening, but she has a very bad case of shingles and she's in a lot of pain," Grace replied.

I remembered a friend who'd had shingles and how painful it was. Shingles is a viral disease that inflames the nerve endings. It is rarely, if ever, fatal, but my friend had lost her eye to it as it raged like a prairie fire across her face and down her body in patches of small, red blisters.

"I'll make arrangements to come as soon as I can," I told Grace. "By the way, how's Dad?"

Dad was very ill with emphysema, and had been for years. It was now called "farmer's lung" by many Midwestern farmers. They'd handled pesticides for years before they knew the chemicals were harmful. Dad had once demonstrated to me how he'd mixed the chemicals by hand in large bushel baskets and told me that the dust would rise up around his face as he stirred the ingredients together. Mom had been taking care of him for years.

"He's about the same," Grace said.

When I got off the phone, Tanya was up and already banging cabinet doors. She did not like being awakened, especially by my family. I knew she'd overheard me tell Grace I'd be going to Minnesota soon to see my mother. Tanya was not pleased.

"You haven't been close to them for years," she reminded me. I knew there was more to Tanya's objection than that.

We rode to the airport in silence. Once there, however, Tanya kept asking, "Do you really have to go? Do you really have to leave me?"

It became very difficult. As I walked away, I looked back to see Tanya crying. I stood around the corner so she couldn't see me, though I could see her reflection in the glass partition. I watched as her shoulders started to shake from her sobs. The stewardess waved at me. I would be the last person to get on the plane. "You have to come now. Hurry!" she said.

I turned and walked toward the door. I was so torn. Was I really abandoning her? I couldn't get the picture of Tanya's shaking shoulders out of my mind.

The first few days with my mother were very difficult. She was in such pain. I had learned a remedy from my friend and it gave my mother some relief. I mixed a huge batch of baking soda with water and applied it all over her. This blocked out the air and relieved some of the pain and itching caused by the sensitive, tingling nerve endings.

It was very difficult thinking about Tanya. I called her often. She would say how much she missed me, then beg me to come home. She also wanted me to say how much I missed her and loved her, but I felt I couldn't say that out loud with my parents around. Finally, I started placing the calls late at night after they had gone to bed.

I was caught between feeling a duty to be in Minnesota with my mother and my desire to be in Honolulu for Tanya. I could still see her shaking as I walked on the plane. I was not there to protect her. Nor could I stop her words from ringing in my ears: "Must you leave me? Please don't leave me."

I thought back to the time I'd gone up the mountain in Switzerland—the last mountain I'd climbed—and her words, "You left me! You left me!" rang again in my ears.

But now that I was in Minnesota, I decided to see if I could improve my relationship with my parents. I had distanced myself from them years before.

"Mom, I'm really concerned about you," I said as I sat down next to her on the sofa. "Do you have any idea how you might have gotten shingles?"

"No, dear, none," she said emphatically with her usual Midwestern stoicism.

"Well, I know they're often connected with stress," I said, taking her hand. "Has anything been bothering you?"

Dad looked at us both, bored with such trivia, and began to head toward the door. "I'm going to get the mail," he said.

As soon as he'd gone out the door, my mother became very animated. "I've got to tell you about the Bowmans who live next door." It was clear she did not want my father to hear what she was about to tell me.

My parents had left their farm years earlier and were now living in an apartment complex for retirees. I had gone to school with the Bowmans' daughter, and I'd envied her because she was so popular and pretty.

"It's terrible," she went on. "He was in such pain from shingles, he killed himself." My eyes widened. "That's right—he committed suicide, and poor Mrs. Bowman found his body on the bathroom floor. He'd shot himself. She was so distraught that before the police got there, she'd already started to clean up the blood and had put the gun away."

Before she could tell me much more, Dad was back with the mail.

I thought about it for a long time. Shingles is a non-contagious disease, yet it had jumped from the apartment next door. Then I realized that Mom had taken on the disease to distract my father from the neighbor's suicide.

Dad's father, my grandfather, had committed suicide when Dad was a little boy. He'd taken poison, and gone down to the pasture to die. When Dad went down to get the cows, he found him lying there. I hadn't been told about it until I was in my late teens, and Mom had always tried to protect Dad from his own feelings. The suicide was an untouchable subject, and now she was trying to protect him from that subject again.

Knowing all this pulled forth a compassion for my parents that I hadn't felt in years, and I wanted to become closer to them.

After I divorced Madison, I didn't remarry or have a long-term relationship with anyone. My parents worried that I had no one in my life. I wanted to tell them that I did now, that I had Tanya. I knew it was a risk, that they might not understand, that they might even disown me, but after my self-imposed distancing from them for so many years, I felt, what have I got to lose?

Over lunch, I decided to risk it.

"Well, you see, Mom, Dad," I began slowly. "Those years of roaming and floating, and your worrying about me are over . . . I've found someone special." I searched for a way to tell them that my someone special was a woman.

Finally, after several stumbling starts, I just reached in my wallet and pulled out a photo of Tanya and me. We were standing near the ocean, our arms around each other.

"This is my soul mate. This is Tanya," I said, putting the photo down on the table between them. "Well, you know what I'm trying to say."

"No, Marilyn," my mother said. "I don't know what you're trying to say." A frown crossed her forehead.

"Well," I mumbled, "Tanya and I are a couple. We share everything. We want to spend our lives together."

My mother lowered her head and began to shovel food in her mouth. My dad, usually the silent one, stopped eating and began asking me all kinds of questions. Finally, he said, "Marilyn, try as I can, I can't think of myself with a man."

I knew how hard he was trying to put himself in my shoes, and I loved him for it. I touched his arm gently and said, "I can't picture you with a man either, Dad," and we both laughed.

Finally Mom looked up from her plate. I knew she was ready to speak, that she had kept quiet so she could listen and formulate an opinion. "Well, Marilyn," she said, "love is love!" Then she added, as if she knew of my other life in the castle, "It can reach beyond the grave."

Much later I went to the phone to call Tanya. It was very late, after ten in Honolulu, but the phone just rang and rang. She should have been home, but I didn't really worry. I knew I would be returning to Honolulu the next day.

As I was walked out the door to go to the airport, the neighbor, Mrs. Bowman, grabbed my arm. Her frail, bone-like fingers were like a vise as she held on to me.

"I had to do it, I had to do it," she said to me. "He was having an affair. Do you know what it's like to live with someone for fifty years and know they're in love with someone else?"

Finally, Mrs. Bowman released my arm. I looked into her misty eyes that were clouded with at least eighty years of living, and I saw her deep pain. I put my arm around her frail shoulders and held her. I realized she'd just told me she'd murdered her husband. I knew she felt she couldn't tell anyone who lived there, and yet she had desperately needed to tell *someone,* so since I was only visiting, she'd told me. I decided I didn't need to tell anyone else.

Some months later when I was talking to my brother, Dustin, he told me that they'd taken Mrs. Bowman away. "To a home," he said. "The police think she probably killed her husband, but they aren't going to do anything about it."

"Yes," I replied, "that's probably a good idea." I knew I didn't envy Mrs. Bowman's daughter anymore.

Chapter Twenty-one

At the Edge

The plane was approaching Oahu. I always took a window seat so I could look down at the island I loved so much. The ocean was an azure blue. The mountains were a deep blue-green as I watched the cumulus clouds pass over them.

As we neared Honolulu, I watched the shoreline and followed it until I caught sight of the area where Tanya and I lived. My eye then followed the street up the hill to our house. The plane cast a shadow over our home as if it were an omen.

Tanya was there at the airport to meet me. She did not have a *lei* for me. I was sorry we'd given up the wonderful Hawaiian custom, but some time earlier Tanya had said that I traveled too much for us to keep it up.

"I'm so glad to see you, honey," I said, throwing my arms around her and being more open with my affections in public than I'd ever been.

"Hi, Marilyn," Tanya said, pushing my arms away. "We are in public, you know."

I gathered my luggage and Tanya went to get the car from the airport garage.

On the drive home, Tanya asked, "How's your mother?"

I began telling her, but before I could finish, she had reached for the radio and switched it on.

After that, we drove along in silence. I had meant to tell her the story about Mrs. Bowman, but it seemed it would crack the stillness between us, and I didn't know if that might further provoke Tanya's obviously bad mood.

When we got to the house, Tanya left me with the luggage as she walked inside. I knew she was upset with me for having been in Minnesota so long.

Days went by and we hardly spoke. Each time I tried to approach her she would turn away from me. I was beside myself with loneliness and I had no idea what to do or how long this would go on.

Tanya soon moved her things into the other bedroom. She explained she had to work so many hours now, often into the evening, and she didn't want to disturb me.

Her behavior was what was disturbing me. We began to live like sisters. No, that's not accurate. There wouldn't be this much distance between sisters.

She had moved the portrait to the hallway, where I had to pass it several times a day as I went to my bedroom. One evening I stood before the portrait for a long time and began to talk to it as was becoming my custom. Her pale green eyes stared back at me as I asked, "Tanya, what's going on with you now? Where are our tangled lifetimes together leading us?"

Tanya was working late many nights. I tried to talk to her. "It isn't good for you to work all the time. You're wearing yourself out," I had said, but she only became angry with me and would walk away.

I thought she was headed toward burnout. I'd read about its signs: anger, impatience, and irritability. There was something else bothering me, but I couldn't quite figure out what it was. I was becoming more and more lonely. I felt like I was living in the house by myself, or at least only with a portrait.

I didn't have many friends left. When Tanya and I had first gotten together, we had vowed our fidelity. She said that she didn't like a lot of my friends, so I stopped calling them.

With most of the friends Tanya and I shared, she had created a triangle, with herself always in the center. And there was always her unspoken demand that we pivot around her, similar to the Queen's demands in the other lifetime.

I was so very tired, so very sad when I went to bed that night. When I awoke in the morning, I grasped at the threads of a dream that had awakened me and wrote it down.

I'm standing on a hillside, washing my car. I continue to wash it as if it won't come clean. I see Tanya driving by with another woman. They're laughing together. I continue to wash the car, but it still won't come clean. In the dream, I realize Tanya is having an affair with the other woman.

Tanya got home from work very late that night. I was sitting on the patio in the dark, the full moon casting long shadows around me. Tanya walked up the steps and gave a start when she saw me sitting in the moonlight.

"Tanya, we must talk."

"I'm too tired."

"No, Tanya, it's very important."

She just stood there.

"Tanya, I believe you're having an affair."

"Oh, Marilyn, where did you ever get that idea?"

I wanted to tell her *from a dream*, but I knew she would only laugh at that. Instead, I said, "All the signs are there: you're working late, you're distancing yourself more and more from me—I just *know* it inside."

She looked at me again. "No, Marilyn you're wrong—you're just having one of your moods." Tanya was always trying to convince me I was moody.

I thought back to the dream: *washing the automobile and it just wouldn't come clean.* I saw the moonlight catch Tanya's colorless green eyes and I thought, *She just won't come clean.*

The days grew into weeks, but nothing changed.

One night while I was waiting for her to come home and sitting there alone, as I did now most evenings, I got up and walked to the portrait and sat down in front of it.

I looked at her pale green eyes staring back at me and then at the pink lapel that formed a triangle. I began to drift, drift, drift into the triangle, thinking, *Is this what I'm in, another triangle?*

As I thought about these triangles, the warm liquid formed around my eyes.

Stone walls surrounded me. I looked down to see a deerskin tunic on my body, leather boots on my feet, and I found myself walking down the hall where flaming torches cast shadows across the castle wall.

As I walked along, listening to the sound of my boots on the rough stones of the corridor, I reflected back to my actions only moments ago in this past life.

I had signed the Queen's portrait and then stepped before her. I had then fallen on my knees while taking her hand into mine. It was so difficult to look into her pale green eyes, feel such desire for her and yet know I had to tell her I was leaving the castle. I just couldn't go on any longer being only one of her many lovers. Jealousy was consuming me and becoming as strong as the passion I felt for her. Days before, I had realized that the look on her face in the portrait had begun to reflect my anger: it had started to grow cold, so I had to stop painting it. Today I had signed it as it was.

"Your Highness," I had said, "your royal portrait is finished. I love you desperately, but I must leave the castle."

Still deep in thought, I continued down the corridor. I lifted my hand to the side of my face. It still stung from where the Queen had pulled the hair from my beard when I told her I was leaving. Her eyes had turned so cold. They had become like pale green cylinders of ice.

I walked on, still rubbing the side of my face. As I passed the archway that led to the turret that the Queen and I had climbed together so many times, I decided to take one last look at the country-side—her world—from the turret. I climbed the circular steps and walked out onto the turret. The entire countryside was before me, but its magnificence had now dimmed. This is the Queen's world, I thought, it is not mine.

I looked below at the velvet green forest, knowing I would soon be walking through it as I left the castle. I leaned over the turret edge to get one last glimpse of the bridge that crossed the moat, which I would soon walk over as I left the Queen.

I did not hear the footsteps behind me.

Suddenly I feel hands at my back. They're pushing me. I try to turn, but it's no use. I'm being pushed harder—and harder.

I hear a long scream.

"Nooooooo—!"

I realize it's my own voice and I'm falling—falling—falling—and then—there is only darkness—and *peace*.

Back in this current lifetime I was still sitting in front of Tanya's portrait, and was once again surrounded by darkness—not the dark-ness of death, but nonetheless a cold, penetrating darkness. I sat there dazed and trembling, staring at Tanya's portrait that is so like the portrait I'd seen in the castle, so like the portrait I'd painted of the Queen in my other life. I had been her lover in that other life and when I left her, SHE KILLED ME.

For a long while I sat there letting the darkness enfold me, reflecting on what I knew of the lifetime when I'd been with the Queen, when Tanya was the Queen, and I wondered if in this lifetime it would happen again, *if I would be killed by the woman with the pale green eyes.*

Chapter Twenty-two

The Wheel Goes Round

Faith makes things possible: it does not make them easy.
—ANONYMOUS

I sat inside the sliding glass doors and watched the wind pick up the leaves and twirl them in patterns as they danced across the patio of our home.

I knew that I *had* lived before. There was no doubt about it anymore, but I also knew that the castle lifetime was only part of the story. In that lifetime Tanya had killed me, and I knew that in this current lifetime it could happen again! All the signs were there, just as they were in the last lifetime: the portrait, the pale green eyes, the triangles, my powerlessness, and the violence. I knew she might not actually kill me physically, though I thought it was possible since I'd experienced her anger and temper, but what really was being killed was my spirit. I felt it was being drained from me.

The leaves whirled across the patio like a wheel, a karmic wheel. *I'm on a karmic wheel*, I thought. It's like a game, like chasing your tail. It goes on and on repeating patterns of triangles and control, or a lack of it. How do I end these patterns of the karmic wheel?

The more intense the strain had become with Tanya, the deeper my faith grew. Where for years I had believed in nothing, I now began to feel there was meaning to it all, that there was something to be learned from the patterns. But how could I find out what it was and how could I break the patterns so I wouldn't be killed again?

I longed to talk to someone about my feelings, but I didn't know who I could turn to. Leilani didn't come around much anymore. I thought of her with her mixed bag of beliefs; I'd have been happy with just one of them.

Then I heard from Jenny. I remembered the fun she and I had traveling together through Europe when we were students. She was coming to Honolulu. "Could we get together?" she asked. "And is it safe to call you Sunshine?"

"Why, yes, of course," I replied, though I don't go by that anymore."

I was delighted at the prospect of seeing her and of thinking about something else besides castles and portraits.

Jenny still had her pixie-cut hairdo and her low-throated laugh. We had great fun reminiscing about our student follies. We laughed about the aging Contessa who'd invited us, along with many handsome young men, to a party on the Grand Canal of Venice. And how when she thought she wasn't getting enough attention, she'd thrown her dress over her head and then leaped into the canal.

A chill ran through my body when Jenny brought up our bicycle ride when we were chased by the German Polizei. I told her I'd never gotten over the fear of Nazi Germany and black boots—and that I almost obsessively read everything I could about the era.

I told her about Tanya, though I did not tell her about the castles, the turrets, and the portraits. I also did not tell her I thought Tanya was having an affair. I knew Tanya would be furious if she thought I was talking about her, let alone telling something so private. I was losing myself, slipping into a powerlessness more profound than I'd ever felt with Madison.

When Jenny and Tanya met, I got the same feeling I'd gotten when Jenny had met Madison: they didn't like each other.

Jenny didn't ask much about Madison or what had happened. She didn't ask much about Tanya, either. She sensed I didn't want to talk about either of them.

Jenny left and I fell into loneliness again.

One evening the phone rang and I reached to pick it up. I already had the receiver in my hand when Tanya yelled from the other room, "I'll get it." I heard her pick up the other phone.

I put the receiver to my ear and heard the voice of a friend of ours, Deborah. I knew she had broken up with her girlfriend some time ago. I heard Tanya purr into the phone, "Hi, sweetie. You know you shouldn't call me here."

I hung up the phone. I didn't want to hear what I now knew was true.

Later I confronted Tanya again.

"You *are* having an affair, aren't you? You're having one with Deborah, aren't you?"

"How dare you—how dare you," Tanya shrieked at me. "You were listening on the phone, weren't you?"

"Then it's true," I shrieked back, my voice breaking. "You're not denying it now, are you?"

"No, I'm not having an affair. You're pitiful. Deborah's only a friend." Tanya's voice had risen above mine to an even higher pitch. "How dare you listen in when I'm on the phone!"

Tanya's face had grown redder and redder. Then she stormed from the room, leaving me trembling and crying.

I tried to gather my composure, but thoughts just kept racing through my mind. She's denied it again—she's having an affair. I thought back to my dream and murmured, "But she just wouldn't come clean!"

Some days later Tanya approached me. "Marilyn, I'm going on a business trip in a few days."

"Where?" I asked. "And for how long?"

"To the East Coast. I'll be gone about five days." Tanya was more animated than I'd seen her in a long time.

"You seem to be really excited about this trip."

"No, I'm not," she said, working hard to lower the pitch of her voice.

I thought it was strange that she was denying her excitement, but even stranger that she *was* excited, since I knew she hated to fly.

While Tanya was gone, I placed a phone call to Deborah's house. I promised myself that I would hang up if she answered. It just rang and rang until a message came on saying she was out of town.

I rang her number three different days. Each time I heard the answering machine playing the same message.

When Tanya returned, I waited until she'd hung up her clothes and walked in the kitchen where I was drying the dishes before I confronted her. "Tanya, we must talk." I paused for a moment trying to gather strength so I could keep my composure, and then went on, "I know what is going on."

"Yes," she replied, seemingly with no emotion, "we do need to talk."

I dried the last dish. My hands were trembling as we walked into the living room and sat down.

"I've tried to avoid telling you this?" she began, "I thought I could work it out." She paused, her bloodless green eyes piercing through the wall I was trying to erect between us. "Yes, I've been seeing someone. I've been seeing her for a couple of months."

I had stopped trembling. I sat in silence for a long, long time. *Nothing* could have prepared me for the shock of what I'd just heard. Even though I thought I'd known it, there was always a part of me that had wanted to believe her when she told me she was not seeing someone.

My mind raced in one direction, then the next. Thoughts crashed over each other. One would begin and before it could reach its conclusion, the next would cascade over it like waves crashing over a sea wall: we were supposed to be soul mates. She's my life. We're supposed to spend the rest of our lives together; we have this karma to work out. Maybe I didn't hear her right. Maybe any moment she's going to tell me she's only joking.

But there she was in front of me. Her words were still ringing in my ears: "Yes, I've been seeing Deborah."

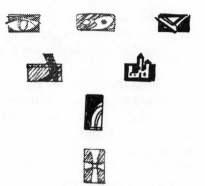

Chapter Twenty-three

Deep Enough to Draw Blood

Tanya sat in front of me, waiting for me to say something. I just sat for a long time. I was numb. I could only remember saying *no* to Tanya once, when I'd said no to the house with the turrets. Now I was about to say *no* again.

Finally, my words came, slowly and deliberately. "Well, then, we're through. It's finished."

"No, no," Tanya said, her voice rising in pitch. "Let me work it through. You can't leave me."

"Tanya, *you've* left *me*."

"No, no, I haven't," she screamed, "I'm still here,"

"Well, you can't have us both. I can't handle it."

I felt as if I was once again in the castle, that I was again turning and walking away, and I wondered, will this kill me this time, too? Will *she* kill me again? I paused for awhile and went on. "Tanya, I thought we had pledged fidelity. I can't handle triangles. I can't stay."

Tanya started pacing back and forth in front of me. "Please, please, Marilyn, I will give her up. Please, please don't leave me."

I just sat there, spent and exhausted, and soon she realized I wasn't going anywhere, and she came over and sat down next to me. She curled her legs under her body and began to stroke my hair, which hung limply at the sides of my head. She told me she would not see Deborah again.

A week later I watched the sun go down over the palm trees in our front yard. Tanya was still not home from work.

When I could no longer stand it, I got in my car and drove down the hill and toward the valley where Deborah lived.

Tanya would hate it if she knew I was spying on her. I felt guilty, as if I were betraying her, her trust, and my pledge to her. I had lost such a sense of myself and was so afraid of losing her, I failed to realize how much *she* had betrayed *my* trust.

I drove past Deborah's house. Tanya's car wasn't there. I rounded the corner to go back home and then I saw it: the silver BMW I had given her. "Why, why?" I said over and over, "Why, why?"

I pulled to the side of the road near her car. I put my head on the steering wheel and sobbed. Her car was there for hours.

I knew Tanya had purposely parked her car around the corner. She thought I wouldn't see it there, but I did, and now I knew the affair had not ended. That she had lied to me again.

I finally drove away. I didn't go home that night, I just drove to the beach and sat watching the dark waves lap endlessly against the shore. I thought of the way Tanya had thrown me from the turret when I walked away, and wondered what she would do to me this time . . . when I walked away.

The patterns were repeating and I felt helpless to stop them. I watched a huge wave crash against a rock, and I felt my life was crashing with it. Another wave followed, and another. Is this like our lives, one to follow another? *Will I be killed again?*

Finally I saw the first, faint rays of the sun breaking across the horizon and I knew it was time to drive home and play out the next act on the karmic wheel.

When I walked up the steps to our house, Tanya was waiting for me at the top of the stairs. Her hair was wild. Her eyes were red.

She looked like an enraged animal.

I was drained and tired and knew I looked like a part of me had gone out to sea with the waves.

"I realize you're still seeing her," I said. "You've lied to me again."

"I couldn't help it," she whined, "I only went to say goodbye."

Another lie, I thought. "No. You're continuing the affair after we had agreed you would end it." There was so little left of me, my voice sounded flat and emotionless. This fueled Tanya's anger and she screamed at me.

"You've got to let me work this through!"

In the lifetime as the artist to the Queen I hadn't even asked for fidelity, nor tried to work it out, but in this one I had. Yet in spite of this slight difference, perhaps even growth of patterns, the deception had happened again. I felt my jealousy and anguish rising.

"Yes," I said flatly and stiffly so I would not break down. "I agree—you should work it through." I drew in a long, deep breath before saying, "But you will not be with *me* while you do."

Her words pelted against me. "You had all those lovers before! You told me you'd known many others! It's my turn now!"

"Yes, but that was *before* I met you." Holding all my feelings just behind my clenched teeth and with the palms of my hands turning white from digging my nails into them so I could keep control of myself, I went on, "It can be your turn, but not while you're with me. I can't stand the triangles. I don't want any part of it." I dug my nails into my palms even harder.

My momentum grew, giving me courage but sapping my control, and I yelled back at her, *"We are finished!* I'm calling Leilani. We're selling the house."

"I'll end it with Deborah!" Tanya had become nearly hysterical. "I'll end it *now!*"

"No, Tanya, I know you won't. Anyway, there's too much sorrow, too much sadness in our lives," I said in barely a whisper, my shoulders dropping from my spent energy. "It's time for it all to be over." I shook my head and said through still-clenched teeth, "IT IS OVER!"

She screamed at me again, "But, but it was only an affair!"

I tasted the salty tears running down my cheeks. "Yes, it was only an affair, but the thing that hurts the most is not the affair, but that you lied to me. I knew long ago you were having an affair. I even dreamed about it. All my instincts told me it was going on and *you* kept telling me it *wasn't."*

I wiped at my tears and went on. "I think I could have handled the affair, but you told me I couldn't trust my own instincts and feelings. When you lied to me, I wanted to believe you. I listened to you—*and doubted myself!"*

Tanya fell in front of me, begging. "Please don't leave me, please don't leave me, Marilyn. Please don't abandon me. You're my *family."*

This took me aback—could we be family? Were we karmic family? I looked at Tanya's red-rimmed eyes and said, "Tanya, there's more history to our relationship than you know about."

I'd never been able to tell Tanya about the castle, the turrets, my other lives, or my beliefs that I had lived before. She didn't believe in reincarnation and she would only have made fun of me.

Tanya believed in nothing. The woman I had once thought was going to save me, the woman who had once had such deep beliefs, had lost them all while mine had been growing and growing.

Finally, I put my arms around her and said, "Tanya, you must face it—it is over."

She broke loose from me, her green eyes flashing. Her fingers grabbed out at my face. Her nails dug deep into the sides of my jaw as she shrieked, "No! No!" with a viciousness I'd never seen before, not even that night in Lucerne when she'd knocked me out.

The sides of my face throbbed with pain as I grabbed her wrists and pulled her hands loose from my jaw. I saw blood on her fingertips and knew it was mine.

I thought, *I'm leaving you, but this time I won't let you kill me.*

I walked from the room and left Tanya weeping on the floor. The sight of my blood on her fingertips had even shocked *her* and she didn't come after me.

The next day, I called Leilani. She didn't ask any questions. She only said, "Yes, I'll list the house. I'll sell it for you."

Chapter Twenty-four

On a Hillside

We got the house cleaned and ready to show to prospective buyers. I had gone up the hillside behind the house and picked magnificent sprays of bougainvillea, brought them down, and placed them all around the garden and the house. The house had never looked more beautiful, and it only made me sadder that I would be leaving this place I had once loved.

Leilani was coming over at 2:00 P.M. for our first open house. As we agreed, she would show the house between 2:00 P.M. and 5:00 P.M.

Leilani was always on time. She said she would come at 1:30 to put up her signs, put out her brochures, and make sure everything was ready.

I looked at my watch. It was 1:45, then it was 2:00. Leilani still had not arrived. I waited five more minutes and called her house.

Her ex-husband answered the phone.

"Is Leilani there?" I said, "We were to have an open house here today and she's the agent showing it."

There was a long pause, a long silence, and then he said, "You haven't heard?"

I felt chills pass through my body. "No, no, what?"

He paused again, then said, "I'm sorry to tell you this over the phone—Leilani's dead."

I couldn't contain myself. I screamed.

He waited a moment, then said, "I'm so sorry to tell you this way. I thought you would've read about it in the newspaper."

"No, no," I said. "I haven't read a newspaper all week."

"Well, Leilani had gone to a broker's open to see a house on the Pali. From what we can piece together, she'd parked her car on the steep hillside. When she came back to her car, it had stalled. She had been the last one to leave and no one else was around. She must've planned to move it herself, but somehow she was behind the car when it started to roll. Her car rolled over her. The authorities think she may have lain there quite a while before someone found her. There were scratch marks all over the ground around her."

I got off the phone. Tanya was standing there, looking at me. She knew better than to say anything until I was ready to speak.

I looked at Tanya and thought, *Could there ever be any moment when I could be sadder?* Tanya was only watching me. Finally I turned to her and said, "Leilani is dead—the Night Stalkers got her."

Chapter Twenty-five

A Second Time

A week passed. I could not shake my sadness. I called Deliah. She and I had only recently become friends, yet we felt as if we'd known each other forever and without the heaviness of karma. Deliah, who was quite psychic, had become like a spiritual adviser to me. I had turned to her the night I heard about Leilani's death and she'd listened to my pained sobbing for hours.

Deliah was a woman whose inner strength shone larger than her frail frame would suggest. Dark, deep-set eyes stared intensely from a narrow, bird-like face and gave a hint of the gems of philosophy that would come from them more than from her thin, taut lips. I had thought that clouds were reflected in her blue eyes until one day I looked at the sky and there weren't any clouds yet I saw the same misty cloudiness anyway.

I could tell her about the castles, turrets, pale green eyes, and triangles, and we would discuss them all as bleed-throughs into my other lifetimes.

"I'm sure there's something I'm supposed to learn from all of this," I said one day when I was nearly paralyzed with pain, "but I feel all the lessons are eluding me."

"Marilyn, you'll find your answer when you're ready—and you're right, we do have flashbacks into other lifetimes for a reason, but they only start to surface when the patterns from that lifetime are beginning to affect this one. They appear so we can recognize them and do something about them."

"Well, why couldn't I get a day in a daisy field?" I pouted.

Deliah laughed. "We rarely go into a memory or flashback of a day in a daisy field. The lessons from that time have already been handled."

"Then I suppose we only meet and get involved with people when we have something to work through with them. Can't people ever find each other and have a good relationship?"

"Yes, sometimes they can when they've had a previous loving relationship without controlling behavior, or when they're both willing to leave their past patterns. Karma is always a control issue: "You owe me, I owe you—and we've got to work it through!"

"Don't we ever meet people we don't *have* any karma with?"

"Yes, we meet them all the time and are attracted to them—people we've known before but never gathered any stuff with, like you and me. We love being with them, but unless we've really let go of most of our own past patterns and karma, we rarely get involved with them. Just for that reason—*we have nothing to work out.*

"Have you ever noticed how often people will choose someone that is just like the last person they were with and that their relationships, one after another, *run the same patterns?*" Deliah paused, then added, "Sorry, no daisy fields again."

Deliah's pause had given me some time to think and find my voice.

"Deliah, don't you think a lot of those behaviors are from childhood?"

"Yes, they can be patterns that were formed in this lifetime—certainly there can be multi-factors operating—but sometimes they run so deeply there has to be another explanation, and that explanation is found in patterns and problems we've brought with us from other lifetimes."

"There, you mentioned problems again—and I'm still looking for my daisy field." I paused and started retreating inside as I added, "Leilani was once a daisy field for me." I then slipped back into my gloom.

"But now she's dead—and I'm lost! Oh, I'm sorry, Deliah, I didn't mean to cut you off, but I'm *so* discouraged."

"It's alright, Marilyn. I know with all that's happened this is such a hard time for you." Deliah put her arm around my shoulder.

"Try to believe in yourself again, Marilyn. Trust that *everything is happening the way it's meant to,* and *believe* and *trust* in your instincts."

"But they've been so *wrong*," I began to protest. "Maybe they're damaged now because I didn't listen to them. Is that why I can't feel them now?"

"Instincts can't be permanently damaged—they're still there for you."

"Oh, I don't know, Deliah I was so mistaken, for so long. Maybe if I could get away, maybe if I could retrace some of my steps . . ." Deliah's talk of breaking patterns had sent a small ray of light flickering through my mind. Maybe I could make some sense out of it if I'd go back to where it began, if I'd spend some time in Europe . . .

Someone else from Leilani's agency was showing the house and arranging for its sale. I renewed my passport and began all the preparations to go abroad. Then, in my desperation to find myself and to escape the constraints of the sadness that engulfed me, I spontaneously sold or gave away two-thirds of everything I owned.

Tanya was like a small, wounded animal. She tried to follow me everywhere, always begging, "Please, please don't leave me."

When I told her I was leaving for Europe, and that I might even move there, she begged to come with me. "Please let me go with you—we can start over."

"You never liked Europe," I reminded her. "I just have to get away from all this sadness," I said as I walked to my car.

I then drove down to the ocean where I could watch the waves lap against the shore. It had become one of my favorite things to do lately, as if the foaming, churning waves could carry some of my pain out to sea with them.

I thought back to the day I'd watched the wind swirl the leaves outside the sliding glass door at our house, the day I knew so strongly I was chained to a karmic wheel along with Tanya.

If I were to walk away now, would it release me from this prison of karma, or would I simply carry it with me? Would I carry small and powerless feeling into another relationship, and another, as I'd carried it from Madison and then to Tanya? But wait—I'd had a past life with Tanya, I'd even re-experienced part of it. Yes, but that didn't seem to help. I still didn't understand what I was to learn.

And then, like a vision spreading across the waves, I saw a huge chain. One link connected to the next—to the next—until the chain stretched out of sight. I knew this lifetime was just one of those links and I also knew I had to continue my search for the way to break this chain or end it. But clearly, I could not run from it. It only would follow me.

I rolled up the window of the car, started the engine, and began the drive back to Tanya. I decided we would have to work it out together.

Tanya welcomed me back. She swore everything would work out.

"This time it will be different," she said. "This time we can go to Paris and have a *real* honeymoon—we can fall in love all over again."

I nodded my head in agreement. A deep part of me wanted it to work out. The naive and ever-hopeful wounded child in me wanted to think we could start over that maybe we could find some happiness; the philosopher in me wanted to think, maybe this time we can handle our karma!

But Paris didn't help my sadness. As I walked the familiar streets, my grief only grew worse. I wasn't even sure anymore where the sadness was coming from. It felt like it mixed and stirred inside me until it became one large black mass. I missed Leilani so very much.

Time after time, in my mind, nightmarish thought haunted me and I would see scenes of what might have happened to Leilani. Pictures of her behind her car, it rolling down the hill, coming toward her, hitting her, rolling over her. How she must have felt as she saw *her own* car come toward her. The pictures would become so real, so terrifying, I'd try to push them away. Moments later they'd come back, even *more* real and terrifying.

How long had she lain there before she died? How could it have happened? How, *how* could this have happened? Did she suffer? How long did she lie there before someone came? Were the scratches on the ground hers, or from something else? The pictures rolled endlessly through my mind.

I knew that what Leilani had feared the most had finally happened to her, that the Night Stalkers had finally gotten her. I guess I'd always known they would, that it was just a matter of time after she had cursed them.

Tanya was also having a hard time in Paris and I knew a lot of it was because of me. I wanted to be alone a lot. I would go out walking by myself so I could be with my own thoughts.

Finally one day, my sad eyes looked at her sad eyes, and I said, "Let's leave Paris."

"Good," she said softly. "Finally!"

I suggested we catch the train to Assisi. St. Francis walked in this walled city in northern Italy. I'd had a romance with Assisi ever since I'd first seen it, and I always felt there was something familiar about it, though I felt sure it wasn't where I'd been tortured during the

Inquisition. I knew that someday I'd have to deal with the Inquisition death and felt Madison had probably been the Inquisitor.

One thing I had gotten in touch with was that after I'd died in the Inquisition, and after I died when the Queen threw me from the turret, I'd gone into the same darkness and then the same peace. So, flashing back into these past lives and remembering parts of them was the first time I'd known or thought of death as a peaceful experience. I'd always thought there would be pain at death just as there was so often before it, but now I knew that death was actually peaceful.

Even though I felt I hadn't died in Assisi, there seemed a familiarity with the monks there. Watching them walk in their long robes, I wanted so much to join them on a stroll through the narrow cobblestone streets and under the arches. Surely I had walked with them before in another life!

Walking alone through the ancient city, I noticed an old church and went in. It was nearly dark inside, except for a window near the front of the church. I noticed that one particular section of the stained glass was blood red. There was a huge cross in front of the window. It bisected the crimson panel so that the sunlight shining through this section twisted down to the floor and formed a deep red triangle.

I walked over to where the triangle pattern of light reached the floor and stared down at it. It was just how the light hit the floor in the flashback of my life during the Inquisition. As if being drawn into another time, and with no control over it, I sat down on the hardwood bench directly in front of where the light hit the floor.

Instantly, the feeling of warm liquid formed around my eyes. *Oh no, not again.*

I looked intently at the blood red triangle of light on the floor at my feet. I was now wearing heavy leather sandals and a long, coarse robe, with a cord tied loosely around my waist. My hands throbbed with pain.

A red-tipped poker came closer and closer to my eyes. A large, thick hand held the long metal rod. I heard a deep, rough voice curse and condemn me. I looked up and saw the *pale green eyes*. They stared at me with rage and anger. The poker came closer and closer.

I heard a voice calling my name, jolting me back to the present. "Marilyn, Marilyn, I've been looking everywhere for you!" I shook my head to clear away the warm liquid that was now receding from around my eyes. As the blur lifted, I saw *pale green eyes.* The pale green eyes of . . . Tanya.

Those were Tanya's eyes at the Inquisition. She was a man in that lifetime—she was the Inquisitor—and she killed me! I'd always thought they'd been Madison's eyes, but now I realized they were actually Tanya's.

"Oh no," my voice screamed from within, *"She killed me twice."*

Chapter Twenty-six

A Falling Star

As we crossed Europe, Tanya grew even more restless. There was very little of Europe she could control and certainly very little of *me* she felt she could control anymore. Meanwhile, a dichotomy was brewing within me. At times I seemed to have an inner strength I'd never known before, perhaps being fueled by knowing I had lived before. Then I would remember that Tanya had already killed me in two other lifetimes and I would become afraid of her.

We shared less and less during our travels. There seemed little of Europe Tanya was enjoying or wanting to see. I suggested we take the train to Holland.

"I want to see the Anne Frank House in Amsterdam. I have some unfinished business with the loft where she and her family hid," I explained. "We only need to spend one day there."

Tanya agreed and we got on the train at Milan to begin the day-long journey across Germany. It seemed it would never end. The train rattled from side to side; sometimes the clatter of the wheels was the only thing that broke the silence. My back was throbbing, on the lower left side where the black-and-blue mark had appeared so many years ago when I met Tanya. All these years, my back had remained weak.

Tanya sat across from me, looking out the window into the sunless sky. She appeared like a helpless child engulfed by the shadow world of the window's reflection. I finally had to look away—it was only making me sadder.

I had no intention of getting off the train in Germany. This time I wasn't going to look for the castle with the portrait. I was living it.

As the clatter of the wheels built a cadence, so did my thoughts. Tanya had killed me twice. What was I supposed to learn from this? How could I make the events different this time? They just kept repeating, even though they were slightly altered each time. And still the patterns would repeat. What did I have to do to change the patterns? If I could make major changes to the events, I could change the patterns and I wouldn't have to be killed again. But how do I do this? And do I have to change the patterns—*or do I have to break them?*

We arrived in Amsterdam as the sun was sinking low in the sky. It was too late to go to the Anne Frank House that day, since the museum and the loft closed at 5:00 P.M. I picked up a guide book and saw that it was also closed on Sundays and Mondays. Today was Saturday, and I just didn't have the heart to ask Tanya to wait three days for a museum to open. My spirits sank even lower. I wouldn't get to go through the Anne Frank House or its loft, nor would I get to explore or heal the remnants of the feelings that remained from when I was in my *own* loft in Minneapolis so many years ago, while I waited for the S.S. Captain, the storm troopers, and the black boots to break down my door.

I had thought I could dispel some of my sadness if I could walk through Anne Frank's loft and gaze out the window at the stars as she had done, but I had told Tanya we would only be staying the night. I really wanted to tell her I wanted to wait until the museum opened, but my sense of powerlessness had become so great I knew I would not. I realized it was not only my back that was now weak, but my resolve.

I hailed a cab. "Could you take us to some small bed and breakfast on the canal?" Maybe that would at least give us some feel for the city of Amsterdam.

We drove through the streets for some time. I had no idea where we were going, but I liked riding along the canal. Evening lights flickered on everywhere I looked, giving an almost magical feel to the city.

I wondered what it must have been like to live there. It may have been exciting at one time, but then I thought of the confinement of Anne Frank and her family and friends in the loft during the war and I began again to be drawn into my feelings of terror around the Holocaust.

I shuddered, remembering how the door to the Franks' self-imposed prison was finally broken down and they were all dragged off to a concentration camp.

The cab driver pulled to the curb. "Here, I think you will like this hotel. The people are very nice," he said.

I pulled myself from my reverie to see a narrow, charming, three-storied building squeezed between many other similar buildings. A small lamp glowed from above the door and cast a yellow light across the inn's front steps.

"Yes, we have something available, a room on the top floor," the clerk said as we entered. "It's very large and has a window, so you will be able to see the stars tonight."

While I was filling out the registration papers, Tanya walked into the small dining room to the left. It was clear she was not comfortable in Amsterdam, nor had she been in any of Europe.

The staff fixed us a small meal of hard-crusted bread and smoked salmon and gave us fruit and cheese for dessert. We sat amongst the dark antiques of the dining room and ate in silence. It reminded me of the silent meals I'd eaten with Gisela and her husband, the S.S. Captain, so many years ago in Germany.

As we climbed the three flights to our room, I wondered if this was anything like the room and the loft that Anne Frank and her family lived in all those years.

From the bed, I could watch the stars through the loft window. I lay awake for hours thinking how this must be like the window *she* looked out when she watched the stars that were her only contact with the outside world. I saw a falling star and closed my eyes to go to sleep as I thought, *The only contact with the outside world.*

The next morning, as we prepared to leave, I was grappling with the luggage as Tanya ran ahead to hail a cab. As I stepped from the door and glanced down the street I noticed that all the buildings looked alike, except that each one was painted a different color. The morning light caught something shiny on the building next door. I looked more closely and saw that it was a bronze plaque. I climbed the steps to see what it said and read, THE ANNE FRANK HOUSE.

Tanya was yelling at me, "Come, come! I have a cab!"

I walked slowly, numbly. We had traveled halfway across Europe.

I had learned Tanya had been my killer in a second life, and now I had discovered I'd actually stayed next to the Anne Frank loft. Certainly it all sounded fated!

Yes, it had been *her* stars I had watched from the loft, yet I was so emotionally drained I wondered whether the star that had fallen was *her* star, or was it *mine?*

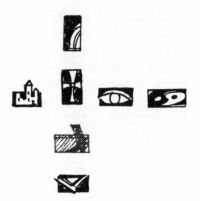

Chapter Twenty-seven

An Angel

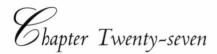

*When angels and saints appear among us, they don't appear
in rich men's houses . . . and the place I want to be, is
where the angels are not only present, but sometimes visible . . .*
                                    —THOMAS MERTON

On the train back to Paris, I plunged more deeply into my own mired
sadness, thinking about the triangles, the affair, and the fact that
Tanya and I never touched. We rarely even talked anymore. Sometimes I wondered which of us was sadder, which of us more lost,
and then . . . WHY, WHY . . . am I still with her? Is this how it will
be forever? Is this the unending links of the chain I saw on the waves?
Will we always be karmically tied together in one death after another?

   As my gloom grew deeper and deeper, I thought that maybe she
had already killed me again, killed my spirit: *I felt like I was no longer
alive.* Then I began to think about suicide. Maybe I should kill myself
before *she* kills me.

   After arriving in Paris, I told Tanya I needed to be by myself, that
I was going out for a walk.

   I left the hotel and walked toward the Marseilles. I remembered
it was a very tall building with access to the roof. I took the elevator
to the roof, which had a garden, and walked through the roses, not

even feeling the thorns as they tore at my legs. I walked toward the edge.

I stood looking down at the street below, at the gnarled traffic, the gnarled people as they passed each other giving no greetings, at the filth of papers that scattered and blew all over the sidewalks. A breeze touched my cheek and I thought about the day the Queen had touched my cheek as we stood on the turret in that other lifetime. I thought about how Tanya had touched my cheek at the house she'd wanted so much in Honolulu.

I leaned over the edge. It would be a quick fall. Maybe I'd pass into the blackness, and then the peacefulness, as I remembered from my two past-life deaths. Maybe death would be my daisy field.

For a moment I held my breath, for a moment all time stood still. I leaned further out over the ledge, and the wind tugged at my blond hair the way Tanya used to. Maybe it's her hand tugging at my hair now and not the wind. Maybe she's inviting me to jump and go into the blackness.

I leaned further into the wind, further into the hand tugging at my hair. I was about to jump ... there was a frozen moment of time ...

If I do this it would be like she had killed me again! It would be no daisy field, *she would be pushing me off the turret again!* The pattern would be repeating, not ending.

Time ticked softly to the beat of my heart. I stepped back from the edge. There *must* be another way, another answer. Certainly there must be something more for me to learn than to repeat this nihilistic pattern over and over.

I turned away from the edge of the Marseilles and strode silently toward the elevator, rode it to the ground, and walked out into the Paris streets.

I walked for a long, long time. I wasn't sure if I still wanted to kill myself or not. I knew it would only be repeating the pattern and that then I would have to come back and live all over again, find her again, love her again, probably be killed *again,* and *again* and *again* until I could find a way to break the pattern.

I continued to walk and walk until I found myself in the Tuileries. I sat down on one of the forest green benches and began to sob. It was as if my tears would never end. Then, through the blur of the tears, I saw something move.

A long iron fence stretched along the side of the park, only ten feet in front of me. On the other side of the fence I saw a small child waving and trying to get my attention.

I brushed my sleeve across my eyes to wipe away the tears so I could see the child more clearly. It was a young boy. He couldn't have been more than four years old. He was hopping up and down as he continued waving, trying to get my attention. Then he said something in French that I couldn't understand, so I replied, "English—I speak *English*."

He nodded as if to say that he understood that we didn't speak the same language, but he continued to wave and then shouted, "Madam, Madam!"

Finally he put one finger into one side of his mouth, one into the other, and stretched his mouth sideways. Then he made a giggling sound as he crossed his eyes. I stared in disbelief. This crazy, silly child is making a face at me! I burst into laughter.

As I laughed, he began to laugh. Then he started jumping up and down, turning around and around as he jumped, all the while continuing to make his absurd faces. I laughed even more.

I got up from the bench and began to imitate him. I turned in a circle while I jumped up and down. I tried making faces, but I was laughing too hard.

I didn't stop until I was completely exhausted. He also stopped. We just stared at each other and then laughed again.

A woman approached the boy, motioned, and called to him. He turned toward her, then back to me and called out, "Madam, Madam!" and waved as he walked away.

I followed him with my eyes until he was totally out of sight. That was an angel, I thought, an angel sent to me to stop me from crying, to stop me from sadness, to stop me from *committing suicide*. I felt lightheaded and alive, as if a warm radiance had surrounded me and all my pain.

The sunlight danced and glittered between the limbs of the trees and cast golden rays in all directions. I stretched out my arms and began to spin in a circle as I chanted gleefully, "No wonder I love Paris—Paris has angels."

*C*hapter Twenty-eight

Murky Madness

Obviously, to face reality can be frightening.
It makes the necessity for change more real ...

—GAIL SHEEHY
Pathfinders

I walked from the Tuileries to the Musée d'Orsay, the museum famous for Impressionist paintings. I had always loved the Impressionists, but never so much as on that day.

I walked into the huge oval room where Monet's famous paintings of water lilies hang, and was surrounded by their play of shadow and light. I knew that was also what was going on in my life, that I was surrounded by the mired darkness and the illusionary light. I looked from lily pad to lily pad and then began going from scene to scene in my life. I could see the dancing light across the water and then by looking more deeply I could see the gnarled roots that stretched from beneath the pads down into the murky water. I felt like I was reviewing my relationship with Tanya. First would come the play, the dance of light, then very quickly the twisted roots took me down into the murky madness—and I knew the madness of our relationship was growing worse. Finally, I stopped thinking and just sat there.

"Maybe I'll start painting like the Impressionists," I heard myself say. I was so deep in concentration that I nearly jumped from the sound of my own voice. Yes, maybe I'd paint Impressionist scenery and never do another formal portrait of a Queen or anyone else again in my life.

I started walking back to the hotel.

Seeing the paintings of the Impressionists, reviewing how they had controlled the light and the dark and brought order to it all, had given me some hope. I wanted to know more about this study of light and dark. Maybe I could bring some order into the spin of the karmic wheel.

Back at the hotel, I found Tanya seated at the window, staring out into the Paris streets. Was she studying the darkness or the light? Was she the darkness or the light—and had I joined her in whichever she was?

"Tanya," I said, trying to interrupt what felt like the murky darkness I'd just seen beneath the lilies in the paintings, "I'd like to go to Monet's Gardens at Giverny. Would you like to go?"

She unfolded her legs from beneath her body and followed me as I started out the door to the train station.

We caught the train and rode in silence the thirty miles to Giverny. I wanted to tell her about the light and the shadow I'd just seen, but it was too close to what we were living, so I just remained silent. Tanya, who I once thought was my soul mate, was like me, locked in a prison of silence. It wasn't clear to me anymore if one of us was the warden, or if we were both inmates.

At Giverny, I walked around the gardens that Monet had spent so much time tending and painting. I looked down into the dark water and knew I had to begin to straighten out my life.

The lily pads, with the murky water beneath them, reminded me of my life. On the surface sat the lilies—what people see of my life as a successful portrait artist. But beneath the waters lurked the murkiness of Tanya's and my twisted lives. The lilies' twisted, intertwining roots were just like our roots—intertwined from our many lifetimes together and our trying to control one another.

"If there is a way," I muttered to myself, "I must find the bottom, *I must get to the bottom of it*, if I'm going to put an end to our twisted lives together."

I looked out over the pond. The light was shimmering across the water. I watched it dance from pad to pad in an unending, perfect pattern. A huge weeping willow stood there, its reflection splayed upon the water. Why do they call them weeping willows when they're so majestic? Yes, so majestic, but its leaves fell like tears into the water beneath it.

Tanya stood not far away and appeared to be looking at nothing. She looked so small, so lost. She only stood there staring, yet I instinctively knew she was thinking about going home. I caught one last glimpse of the glow of sunlight and knew I wanted to go home, too.

I would start painting landscapes, painting to catch the shadow and light—no, I'd had enough shadow. I just wanted to catch the *light*.

Neither of us had really tried to put the relationship together again while we were traveling. I was still too sad and hurt and Tanya just seemed so lost.

I looked at her again as she stood by a lone, purple iris. The sunlight was reflecting off her soft, brown hair and I felt the pull to my heart and I wanted to protect her, to make her feel all right.

"Tanya," I called softly to her, "let's go home."

It was a long flight back to Honolulu. Tanya's fingers again turned white as she gripped the arm rest. She was still afraid to fly.

Chapter Twenty-nine

A Small Gecko

*Obstacles cannot crush me ... He who is fixed to a star, does
not change his mind.*

— LEONARDO DA VINCI
The Notebooks

Honolulu wasn't home anymore. It felt foreign. It felt strange. Tanya
and I bought an apartment in a high-rise near the beach. I didn't
want to live in a house anymore; I felt it would remind me too much
of our past pathos in our other house.

We now both acted as if we wanted to start over. We began by
taking long walks on the beach. We started going to the theater and
then had deep discussions about the twists and turns of the plot,
but we never discussed the twists and turns of our life together. It
wasn't safe.

Tanya had given up her job when we went to Europe and within
a short while, she got another as an administrator at one of the
hospitals. It required a lot of her time and energy. Our walks on the
beach became less frequent, and we rarely had time to be together
for anything else, either.

I became worried and desperate to figure out how to make our relationship work. How ironic—so many years had gone by, so many lifetimes, and we were still such novices at relationships.

I remembered a friend, Pepper, from where I'd lived in California and I phoned her. Pepper's real name was Martha Pepperdine. With her great wealth, she collected art and had become a patron of my work. Though Pepper was nearly thirty years older than I, we'd developed a friendship.

I knew that Pepper and her girlfriend, Tricia, had been together for nearly thirty-five years. I also knew they'd been through hell during those years. Rumor had it Pepper played around a lot.

When I phoned her, she seemed truly pleased to hear from me.

"Hello, Marilyn, we miss you in California," her low voice boomed over the phone. "When are you coming back?"

"Not soon, I'm afraid." I knew the sadness was escaping from my heart and into my voice. "I'm in a relationship now, and it's with a woman."

This intrigued Pepper a great deal so I soon began to tell her all about the Tanya I loved and felt I needed to be with, emphasizing especially her work and service to others. I thought maybe, since Pepper had spent so much time in a relationship with a woman, she would have some secret wisdom that could shed light on my tormented, volatile relationship with Tanya.

I found myself pouring the sadness of my heart out to her over the next hour, talking as I had to no one else about Tanya. It seemed I really didn't want advice, I only needed to talk.

Finally I had to hang up. I was beginning to feel guilty, as if I had violated the privacy Tanya always demanded. My last desperate words to Pepper were, "If only someone, something could help me. Sometimes I feel so *trapped*."

I hung up, vowing I would not turn to anyone again about Tanya. I knew she would be furious if she found out I had.

Tanya's work began to take more and more of her time, so I decided I should once again think about painting. At first I truly wondered if I really wanted to paint at all. Then I thought of Monet's paintings and decided I would try to paint the light. I set up a small studio in the apartment.

Painting soon became my salvation.

I loved mixing the soft, subtle pastel colors the way the Impressionists did, so I could catch the feeling of light. I would explore ways to weave the colors back and forth, always looking for a way to express emotion, feelings, and the light. I brought back the memories of the light dancing across the water and the lily pads at Monet's home in Giverny and tried to capture the play of that light before it sank into the shadowy water and twisted roots beneath the surface. I tried to avoid the shadow, but I found that in Impressionism, as in life, you must have shadow to contrast the light.

I painted more and more to avoid thinking about Tanya and our relationship. Again, we weren't doing well. Had we ever? Or had we always been aboard the sinking *Titanic*? I had lost so much of myself and Tanya was always so absorbed in her work.

"Tanya," I said one morning as I poured her coffee, "let's go for a walk on the beach when you come home from work today."

"Oh, honey, I think it'll be too late."

"I don't mind, anytime will be okay. I just miss you so much."

"Now, Marilyn, don't be a baby. You know how a new job is. You have to be there," Tanya said as she turned her pale green eyes away from me.

I began to absorb myself in my work, too, finding all my joy, my life, in painting. More and more I found I could capture an inner light in my work, almost as if I could get my paintings to glow in the dark. I was not sure how I created that much light, but I didn't try to analyze it. I was sure it was connected to my deepening belief that there was more to life than the walk-around world.

Sometimes when things became the most difficult, I would call Deliah. She allowed me to explore anything: my feelings, reincarnation, and always, whether I was in a good mood or a bad mood, she would allow me to have the mood and then explore it with me. At times my moods would become very dark. They had once reflected only what was going on with Tanya, but now they had become more reflective of my search for the meaning of life, my spirituality. Tanya didn't like my seeing Deliah, but I did it anyway.

As my inner life expanded and deepened, so did my work. I brought home huge canvases, sometimes as wide as ten feet. They were too big for the studio, so they would end up in the living room. Tanya didn't like that, either, but she wasn't there much. She was working ten to twelve hours a day at the hospital.

I would frequently walk down to the shore by myself and watch the sun set into the ocean. Sometimes as I watched the sun sink into deep, crimson water, I felt I might be sinking, slipping away and disappearing with it.

I had given up my studio at the Hilton Hawaiian Village when I went to Europe, so I had been living off my savings since then. I knew I didn't want another separate studio. And I knew I didn't want to paint portraits anymore.

I began finding myself standing at the edge of the balcony looking down, looking down frequently.

Falling . . . falling . . . falling, as I had done from the turret, didn't seem so foreign anymore and I felt I would welcome the peacefulness that would follow it.

The phone rang. I heard an excited voice on the other end.

"Sunshine, Sunshine, is that you?"

It had been so many years since anyone had called me that. It seemed almost foreign now.

"Yes," I replied in a monotone.

"Sunshine, this is Julie—Julie and Scott from college days. We've been looking for you for years. We're coming to Honolulu. We want to see you."

I wasn't into seeing anyone much anymore, I didn't want people to see my depression, but maybe this would be different.

"Yes," I said, my voice lifting a little, "I'd love that."

Julie and Scott arrived two weeks later. We went out and laughed and played together. It was good to laugh again. I didn't tell them about my flashbacks to other lives or about being killed by Tanya in those previous lives. I couldn't talk about it yet, and I didn't tell them that the edge of the balcony was looking inviting to me. I also said little about Tanya. I knew she would have hated it if she thought I was talking about her. They only saw her in passing. She was always working and never wanted to go out with us.

I often caught Julie and Scott watching me. Could they sense my sadness, my loneliness? Through the years, I'd tried to hide my feeling from everyone. I hid behind my work or laughter or partying. I was afraid if anyone were to see inside me they would find how small I felt.

Near the end of their visit, Scott said, "We've done well financially, and we love your new work." I noticed Julie nodding behind him, a very special sparkle in her eye. "What's for sale?"

"Everything," I said. There were canvases everywhere.

"Good," Scott said as he walked from painting to painting, "I'll have *that* one and *that* one."

Julie joined in, "And we must have *that* one."

Soon I joined them in their enthusiasm and started setting paintings up one at a time for them to look at.

By the time their holiday ended, I could see through the reflection of their eyes that my new work was good and I could finally look in the mirror and smile again. I also backed away from the edge of the balcony.

Much of the time I wasn't feeling too well, and it was more and more difficult for me to handle the large canvases. My back often hurt a great deal, the lower left side throbbing.

When I told Tanya, she just said, "Well, if you don't feel good, go to a doctor."

I went. They took some tests. Then they took some more tests. On the third round of tests, they said, "We need to talk to you."

I thought I was prepared for anything. I wasn't.

"The tests show you have cancer. It's curable." I didn't hear anything after the word "cancer"; I didn't hear the "curable" part. I'm not sure anyone ever hears anything after they hear that six-letter word.

Now I had a new distraction, a distraction that could take my mind off the loneliness, the hurt, and the sadness I still felt from Tanya's betrayal during the affair, and over Leilani's death. Yes, now I had a new distraction: I wanted to live.

I was given a hysterectomy to handle my cervical cancer and was then pronounced cured. The physical part of me was cured, but I'm not sure anything else was. I had hidden my feelings from others for so long. I'd also begun to hide them from myself, so I wasn't sure how I felt anymore.

I walked to the balcony and looked over it, wanting to see if I could find a message floating on the wind.

As I closed the sliding glass door on the balcony, the door caught a small gecko as it scurried along the door frame. The gecko, a tiny chameleon-like lizard, is sacred to the Hawaiians. It dropped to the floor, its tiny body rolled over, and it lay rigidly on its back. It's pinkish underbelly had been ripped open and three tiny, perfectly formed eggs had fallen from it.

I looked at the small creature that now would never give birth, and I burst into tears. Over and over, I said, "I'm so sorry, I'm so sorry!" I thought of the child I had once aborted, and the womb, the nurturing part of me that had become infected by a sick relationship always eating at me and then had turned into cancer. My womb was now gone, and I cried. I cried and I cried for the child I would never have.

Black Marks/Black Signs

The thing I fear most is fear.
     —MICHEL EYQUEM DE MONTAIGNE
     Essays, to the Reader

Things at work were going poorly for Tanya. She would often enter the apartment looking tired and drained. I had watched her become more and more controlling. It was as if she was taking larger and larger bites out of the world around her, all in the desperate hope that controlling everything and everyone would give her a sense of safety.

But the feeling of safety never came, and her inconsolable craving for *that elusive sense of security* drove her to become increasingly domineering. The people at work began to react to her overbearingness.

"Honey, do you want to tell me what's going on at work?" I asked gingerly, afraid of her anger. "I know something is."

"No, I don't want to talk about it. It's enough having to go through it each day!"

"Maybe another perspective would help," I said softly. I wanted so desperately to help her, to protect her.

"There's already too many of those—it's all political infighting," she said as she walked into the bedroom and slammed the door.

Though I couldn't get her to talk about the details of her administrative battles, I could see they were taking a toll on her and her self-esteem.

After one particularly brutal board meeting, she came home and announced she could not take the pettiness of the hospital politics any longer. I looked at the lines that had been recently forming around her clouded green eyes and suggested we leave Honolulu.

"Maybe," was all she said.

Two days later, Tanya walked through the front door at midday and announced, "I'm ready, let's leave Honolulu!" I'm not sure what had happened at the hospital and was too afraid to ask, but she'd clearly had enough.

Now we both had something else to think about. I knew I would miss Deliah and the azure-blue ocean. But I also knew I wanted to get away from some of the pain connected with Honolulu, away from the pain and the memories of Tanya's affair and Leilani's death. Sometimes the memories and the pain would still wrap around me like a brittle, chilling cloak and I could hardly catch my breath.

So we both began to look forward to getting away from Honolulu. After some discussion we decided to move to California and to the coastal city where I'd lived before I moved to Honolulu.

Once in California, we bought an apartment on the twentieth floor in a building on the ocean. We never discussed buying another house.

One of the first things I did was call Pepper. I wanted to see her and I also thought that she and her friend, Tricia, might know some people they could introduce us to. Surely in their thirty-five years together they would have met a lot of interesting people—maybe even some that Tanya would like.

"Marilyn, I'm so glad you're back. We have to get together. I'm so anxious to meet Tanya." Then Pepper said in her very low voice, "Tricia's not well, not well at all. I have to take her to the doctor's now, but I will give you a call later."

By the time we got together the next week, Tricia's condition had deteriorated a great deal. I was deeply concerned for Tricia as well as for Pepper and what she was dealing with. I could see how tired she looked and that her age was showing. Tanya immediately took a liking to Pepper and also showed deep concern for Tricia. I was so pleased that Tanya had finally met friends of mine that she liked. We began to see them often and offered to help in any way that we could.

Soon I began painting again. Tanya found a good job that required her to work twelve hours a day. It seemed all her jobs did.

I worked on painting—painting the shadow and the light. I completely stopped doing portraits. Sometimes I would paint a figure way off in the distance, but it was really capturing the light that interested me. I began a series of water lilies, with light dancing and shimmering off the water. I also painted arches and paths—always paths that led to hope. I felt strongly about one particular painting and wrote a poem to go with it.

I was sitting on the bed rereading the poem when Tanya walked in.

"What's that?" she asked.

"It's a poem I just wrote. Would you like to read it?" I handed her the poem. Her eyes narrowed as she read it.

THE PATH

> There is a path for each of us . . .
> It leads to home
> How will I know when I am on it?
> You will know—it will feel like going home
> When will I arrive?
> There is no arrival, there is only the journey
> The difference is,
> Now you think you journey alone.

"Humph, what does it mean?"

"It's about finding your faith—the road *home!*"

I knew I was deepening and I was finding my faith. The deeper my faith became, the more it seemed that Tanya lost hers.

"Geez—are you still looking for answers? I told you I'd looked through it all and there's nothing."

"Yes, I'm still looking, and I know there is something. I know there is *more*. That's what the poem's about—finding the *more* of life, and the path home."

"Marilyn," Tanya said, shaking her head, "you're such a dreamer. There's nothing!" She paused for emphasis. "When you're dead, you're dead. You turn to dust!"

"I used to think that way, but I don't any longer." I narrowed my eyes as I looked intensely at Tanya. "I think a lot of the pain we feel is *because* we feel separated. That's what the last line of the poem is about—*we think we are alone.*"

I could tell Tanya was becoming angry with me, angry because I *believed*. She started approaching the bed.

"I suppose you even believe in God?" she screamed at me.

"Well, I don't know if there's an individual God, but I know my faith is the most important thing to me."

Tanya leaped on the bed, pushing me hard against the headboard. "Tell me," she shrieked, "tell me, who do you love the most—your *God* —or *me*? Tell me, tell me!"

"Tanya," I yelled, pushing hard against her, *"stop it!"*

"Tell me," she shrieked again. "Tell me, *who* do you love the most?"

"You," I said, knowing I'd *lied!*

The scene in the bedroom felt unreal, but now I realized there had been many unreal scenes with Tanya through the years. She had grown so controlling, so insecure, that she even felt personally threatened by my faith.

I began telling her less and less about my feelings, less and less of my beliefs. The more I drifted from her the angrier she became.

I missed my meetings with Deliah, but occasionally I called her. She always let me explore the spiritual, the path, the hope. She had told me about angels and guides and had assured me that we all have them, that we can call on them for help when we need to.

My past-life flashbacks were still happening. I already knew a great deal about my life in the castle and my life during the Inquisition, so now, I turned my attention toward learning more about World War II, Nazi Germany, and the concentration camps. It had become almost an obsession to watch the many documentaries on these subjects.

I knew there was something I needed to piece together from this obsession, but I had not yet found the key that would unlock my past life in Nazi Germany. I felt there must've been a mass incarnation of souls who'd been involved with the Holocaust since so many others also seemed obsessed by the events surrounding it and would become almost traumatized when it was mentioned. Somewhere inside I suspected that in that life I'd died in a concentration camp and that's why I'd reacted so vehemently at Dachau.

Exploring all the flashbacks with Deliah helped, but it was also helpful for me to explore new paths. I became more hopeful about life.

But as my moods became brighter and clearer, Tanya's began to get lower and darker. Perhaps I had been neglecting her and wasn't there enough for her when she needed me, or perhaps it had nothing to do with me at all and it was only her own inner fears of who she was, and her fear of losing control. Certainly, she was beginning to lose her control over me.

It was a particularly gloomy day at the beach when I received a call from Pepper, telling me that Tricia had just died. I told Pepper I would call Tanya and that we would both come over.

When I arrived, Tanya was already there. Pepper seemed to be handling it amazingly well. She told us it was no surprise, that she'd expected it for some time. I appeared to be more in a state of shock than she was.

I wondered if it would hit her later, or if maybe she was just one of those people who can process things quickly. I told her I would be there for her if she ever needed to talk. Tanya was always good with people when they were hurting, so she stayed behind to console Pepper.

After Tricia's death, and maybe because of it, my search for my soul intensified. I also wondered about the light that people with near-death experiences began to speak of so freely. I turned to my paintings for the companionship I no longer had with Tanya since she was gone so much of the time.

Then, signs began to appear again—signs that Tanya might be having another affair. She began staying at work later and later and she told me less and less about what was going on in her life. But mostly, it was my intuition that told me something was going on. During the previous affair and Tanya's denial, I had ignored my instincts, so this time, I was determined to listen to them—and they were telling me something was very wrong.

The thought of Tanya seeing someone else seemed even more painful this time. We had gone through so much together. I kept telling myself that since we were soul mates, we were learning lessons together that we'd be able to work through . But I also knew I couldn't handle another triangle.

One day I walked to the balcony to look out toward the ocean. Way off in the distance I saw two people walking arm in arm. I could tell they were lovers. I felt like spying on lovers that day, so I swung the telescope around on its pedestal to get a closer look. It was Tanya and Pepper. I stood there in disbelief. There was over 30 years age difference—could they be lovers? As I stared they continued to walk arm in arm. They were walking away from me.

I stood there for a long time. I wondered how many tears I'd have to shed over this woman whom I'd known for at least three lifetimes. How many twisted lives have we had together, how much karma? Would we ever break the karmic chain, would we ever get it right?

Why did I find her again and fall in love with her again, *a woman*, and why was I still with her?

I thought back to the murky water of Giverny and the lilies that just sat there on the surface, like so much of our lives—just surface. But beneath that surface, as in our lives, the murky water was filled with gnarled roots that twisted down, down into the darkness. I was once again in that murky water, and like the roots, I was twisting downward and I had no idea where the bottom of the darkness was. All of my lives with Tanya—every one of those lives—had become like distorted, intertwined vines sinking lower and lower into murky madness.

I called Deliah in Honolulu. I told her how low I was sinking, and that I thought Tanya was having an affair.

"Another triangle, Deliah, and with a woman I thought was a friend."

"You thought Tanya was your friend, too," Deliah said. "I'm not really surprised. This has been her pattern in this lifetime *and in another*. Marilyn, remember your faith—it can help you."

"I think I'm losing that along with my sanity. I don't want to think about any of it, especially the patterns. They always come down to me being killed. I'll probably find out that's what happened in Nazi Germany, too!"

Deliah went on for several more minutes trying to console me. She finally ended with, "Be good to yourself, Marilyn—you'll need it to ride this one through."

When I got off the phone, my back was throbbing with an almost shock-white pain.

I called a masseuse who did healing bodywork and was known for helping people get in touch with the deeper parts of themselves. She could take me immediately. Tanya had not gotten home yet so I drove over to see the masseuse.

She had me lie face down on her massage table and began running her hands over my body. When she moved to the lower left side of my back, I screamed as pain shot through my entire body.

She quickly but gently sat me up and asked, "What is going on with your back?"

"I know this woman. We have a relationship. When I first met her, a black-and-blue mark appeared on my back. My back's been weak ever since." I knew my voice was giving away how furious I really was with Tanya.

The masseuse looked at me and her eyes glazed over as she said,

"You've known this woman many lifetimes, and she has come into your life again. You needed to find her. She has a gift for you."

I shook my head, not wanting to believe what I was hearing. How could this woman, this woman who'd killed me in two lifetimes and abused me in this one, have a gift for me? How could finding her again and then falling in love with her, a woman, be a positive thing?

"You were *born* to find her again," the masseuse went on. "She has a gift for you, the gift of *knowing who you are*. She has come into your life so you can finally know the patterns of all your lifetimes. You must search through these patterns."

She shook her head and continued. "This black-and-blue mark is a very, very special mark for you. Let me show you what it looks like."

How could she know what it looks like if it's no longer there? It had been healed years before.

She went to her desk, pulled out her crayons, and began to draw a black mass in the exact shape of the one I had years before. It was a tall, thin mark, four inches high and very narrow. It was dark and muddy.

"Yes, yes," I gasped. "That's *exactly* what it looked like."

She then grabbed another crayon and began to draw sprays of purple that lightened as they neared the edges of the mass.

"You see," she said, as if a vision was playing out before her, "you can work it out. Though there is a dark mass, there is also light radiating from it. It will dissipate, but this means that for you to work out your karma you must search for the patterns." She looked directly in my eyes and said, "You must look for the meaning of it all."

"Yes." I said, beginning to tremble, "but how do I do that?"

"My suggestion is that you try to meditate on it."

"I will try," I said, but inside I felt a fear and a foreboding deeper than I'd ever felt even during my search into the lifetime of the Inquisition.

When I got back to our apartment I tried to put it out of my mind and I decided to wait up for Tanya. I had a triangle to deal with.

It was late in the evening when I finally heard Tanya at the door. I was sitting in the dark watching the moonlight make strange patterns through the sliding glass doors. The long patterns of light reached across the living room and spread over my body. I just sat there, my hands gripping the arm rest so intently that my knuckles were white.

"Why are you sitting in the dark?" Tanya asked as she walked in. "Do you like it in the dark?"

I looked up. "I feel like I *live* in the dark." I paused, then went on. "You're doing it again, aren't you, Tanya? You're having an affair."

"No, I'm not having an affair. I just have someone I'm very close to whom I need in my life right now."

"It feels and sounds like an affair to me."

"Well, feel what you want—it's what I'm doing."

She walked away from me. I looked at the pattern of light at my feet. It formed a triangle.

That night she moved into the other bedroom. As I watched her move her things, I thought that it really didn't matter since we hadn't had a love life for a long time.

Each day I tried to paint, but it became more and more difficult. I dipped deeper and deeper into the shadow.

Tanya was now openly seeing Pepper, but we still seemed unable to let go of each other. She kept saying, "The three of us can work it out." Several times, she tried to arrange for the three of us to get together to discuss a way we could all live together.

Pepper had called me more than once and said that for Tanya's sake we should find a plan; she assured me that she was working on just such a thing that would include all of us. What kind of plan could possibly make me happy if it included sharing my lover with someone else in some ludicrous arrangement?

I couldn't bring myself to do the meditation the masseuse had suggested. I couldn't concentrate on it, so I would go to the easel instead and try to paint.

One day as I stood before the easel, I felt the warm liquid form around my eyes, and I started to lose my balance.

When I looked down I saw *high black boots on my feet instead of my painting sandals. My white painting smock had turned into a brown shirt.* I heard a chilling scream and knew it had come from my own throat. It pierced through my body and pulled me back to my sandals, back to my white smock and back to my easel.

I raced to the phone. "Deliah, Deliah, you must help me—please help me!"

Deliah listened carefully and said, "Don't be afraid of it. Lean into it—you can handle it. Go in and meditate on it and lean into the experience. Your guides will help you."

"Guides? I'm not sure I even believe in guides right now. I'm not sure I believe in anything at this moment."

"It's all right, Marilyn," Deliah said. "You'll be all right. With karma and flashbacks into other lives you must learn to *expect the unexpected*. We've all had lives in the dark as well as the light. We all have things that are hard to face. Just meditate. Just lean into it. You *will* be all right!"

I got off the phone. My mind raced rapidly. Could I meditate, could I stand it? I didn't know.

For two days, I walked around saying, "I'm not sure I can handle this. I'm not sure I can handle this." My thoughts raced continuously. ". . . black boots, brown shirts . . . No, not Nazi Germany that way . . . *no, not me as a soldier on the other side* . . . I'm painting the *light* now—I can't *handle* the dark . . . no, not the other side of Nazi Germany, not me in black boots . . . *Lord help me!*"

The warm liquid formed more and more often around my eyes, and my disorientation was so tremendous, I finally had to give in. I went in and lay down on the bed to meditate. When my breath had calmed, I slipped further and further into a deeper state. As my breathing started into a soft rhythm the warm liquid formed around my eyes and I went back . . . back . . . back.

Heavy black boots coated with dust covered my feet. I was sweating profusely into the brown shirt that was too dark for such a hot day under the sun.

The town leader had pulled me and some of my schoolmates out of class, and told us we had more important things to tend to.

I lifted the military hat from my head and brushed my blond hair back from my brow. With my sleeve, I dusted off the swastika I was proud to wear as a Nazi youth. I placed the hat back on my head and started marching toward the woods. The commander shouted orders behind me.

Peasants in rough clothes—women and children—were being forced to march in front of us and out into the woods. I knew that this was a special day for all of us: this drill could teach us to gather 'the enemy' to protect our Fatherland. I wondered how women and children could be the enemy, but I knew it was important to follow orders.

Near the edge of the forest, we approached a ditch, but I was too far away to see what was in it. A child stopped at the side of the ditch and then turned around toward me. I looked into her *pale green eyes*. They seemed to pull me into them. I stood as if in a trance.

I know those eyes, I thought. I know them, but from where?

The child stared at me intently. A chill passed through my body.

The *pale green eyes* began to penetrate into me. How do I know those eyes? Where do I know them from?

I could no longer hear the orders of the commander. The pale green eyes were piercing into me and impaling me as if I were under *their* command.

The gun slipped from my hand. I took several slow steps forward. With shaking hands I reached down for the shivering child with the pale green eyes. My delicate hand brushed the hair back from one of her soft pink cheeks. A fire flashed in her pale green eyes, a fire I remembered from somewhere. I held her, cradling her as I tried to remember. I rocked back and forth with her as if the pendulum motion could make time go backward to the place where I first saw those pale green eyes, but I could not remember. All I could do was mumble in a barely audible whisper, "Do not fear, do not fear," to the child I was holding so close.

Her shaking body calmed and the fire grew in her eyes. She was no longer afraid, at least not of me. She was in control. I felt my power being sucked from me. It was as if hers was now the power over life and death. I stood there rocking her for a seeming eternity. I did not hear the orders being shouted behind me, the orders to *shoot or be shot.*

I yelled with pain. White piercing fire shot from the lower left side of my back where I knew a rifle butt had just struck me. A narrow, four-inch-high rifle butt. My hips thrust forward with the brutal hit. Then I doubled over, the child still in my arms. We fell over and over, tumbling down into a dark pit that was already filled with the bodies of women and children who'd been driven into it and then shot.

I was already drifting into the blackness . . . down . . . down as I felt the fire pierce my body once, twice, more . . . as the bullets ripped into me and the last of my consciousness. Then slowly, I went into the black, followed by the peacefulness I'd experienced at the end of every other lifetime as life had drifted from me.

Chapter Thirty-one

Broken Patterns

Life can only be understood backwards; but it must be lived forwards.

—SØREN KIERKEGAARD
Life

I called Deliah in near-hysteria and told her what I'd "leaned into".

She talked slowly and calmly, trying to transfer some of her calm to me. "I'm not surprised at all," she said. "I had a vision of it quite some time ago."

Then I told her about Tanya, Pepper, and the latest happenings in the triangle. None of that surprised her, either. "I didn't need a vision about any of this—I expected it."

Tanya and I hardly even passed each other in the apartment anymore. In spite of everything and the situation appearing nearly hopeless, I had begun to mistakenly think my need for her was actually love. In fact, the cancerous pattern of relinquishing my power had become so pervasive, I felt I couldn't live without her. However, when I tried to confront her with what was going on, she would only say, "You live your life, I'll live mine. A person has a right to their secrets."

"Yes," I said weakly, "but I've always believed that the longer you're with someone, the more honest you will be in a relationship and the more you will share together, not less." I continued, my voice growing fainter, "Everything that's happening is foreign to me, and it doesn't make any sense."

She turned her head away from me and began to file her nails.

Something inside of me started to scream as if I was slipping into madness. I'd always thought that when two people loved each other, they'd try to work together, grow closer, and not develop more secrets between them. Was I going insane or was Tanya asking me to betray all that I'd ever believed? The gloom pulled more tightly around me and I found myself asking, "WHY, WHY, am I still with her? Why do I feel my very survival is being with her. Why can't I let her go?"

Finally she set her nail file down, looked up at me, and said. "If you were big enough, we could work this out. The three of us could all live together."

"So that's it. You want us all under one roof, with you in the middle. Tanya, I hate triangles." Warily, I retreated into my thoughts. God, this is painful. If this is a lesson, what am I supposed to learn from it? Am I supposed to be pliant and let her have whatever she wants? I tried that with the Queen and look what happened.

Tanya noticed my retreat into my inner thoughts and cleared her throat loudly.

"Pepper has some ideas about how it could work. Why don't you call her?"

"No," I replied angrily. "I don't make a good maid."

"You're still my family and I want it to be the three of us," Tanya shot back, still ignoring my anguish. "But with or without you, I'm going to work this one through."

"So am I," I replied, nearly under my breath.

I then retreated once again into my tormented reflections and began thinking of the four lives—past and present—I now knew we had shared. Perhaps Pepper was a part of it, too. Perhaps we were all karmically tied together in some scheme of ritualistic torture. I knew somehow I had to work it through, too, all of it, but I didn't yet know how. Through the haze of my despair, I did know that my plan didn't remotely resemble any of Tanya's or Pepper's ideas.

In final desperation, I called Deliah and asked her if I could come see her in Honolulu.

"Of course," she replied.

Deliah picked me up at the airport. She put a five-strand *pikake lei* around my neck. It made me think of Leilani and how much I missed her. Soft Hawaiian music was playing on the radio as we drove along the shoreline. Looking at the deep, azure-blue water I realized just how much I had missed it all. Deliah pulled the car out at a secluded seawall and stopped so we could talk without being interrupted.

I immediately began to tell her the sequences of past lives I'd run over and over in my head. It was as if I had them memorized. I was beginning to see the patterns, but I still couldn't figure out what I was supposed to learn from all of it.

"It's clear that the Inquisition was our first life together. It was Tanya's pale green eyes that were staring at me, not Madison's as I'd originally thought." I scarcely took a breath. "She gouged my eyes out and killed me. In that lifetime she was a man and I was a woman. In the next life, I was a man—an artist in the court of the Queen—and she was a woman, the Queen. In that life she also killed me. Now, if I were to do an eye for an eye, in the third life I would have killed *her*, but I didn't. In that life I was man, or rather, a young boy, a Nazi-in-training, and she was a child."

My words were spilling out almost faster than I could speak them. "I looked at those pale green eyes and I recognized them. Instead of killing her as I'd been ordered, I laid down my gun and picked her up. Was I trying to recognize who she was or had I really not wanted to kill her? Was I trying to protect her?" I paused only a moment, then went on. "One way or the other, I had broken the karmic pattern—I had not done an eye for an eye—I had not killed her as she had killed me—and so now *our chain was broken.*" I stopped to catch my breath, but also felt puzzled. "Then why this lifetime?"

Deliah was silent as I tried to calm down. She had sat there patiently listening through it all. I paused, looked at her, and finally sighed. "Does any of what I'm saying make sense?"

"It really doesn't matter whether it makes sense or not. What matters is that it's there for you to see. That's what's important."

I continued on, "All right, I see it, but then *what* is going on? Why is this pattern repeating itself over and over? Why can't I break it? Why did I have to find her in this fourth lifetime, when we are both women. Why did I have to fall in love with a woman? Was it the only way the pattern would catch my attention? Well, now that it has my attention, I see it, but what am I supposed to do with it?" I was almost frenzied with my questions.

Deliah looked at me. I could see she was reviewing the entire pattern in her mind. Finally, she said, "Perhaps this time it's to say goodbye."

Now it was my turn for a long pause. The understanding was pouring in. It didn't matter to my soul that she was a woman—that I was a woman. The soul knows no gender, it only knows love and familiarity.

A channel had opened and I now understood: it doesn't matter when people meet what sex they are or what role they are playing— father, mother, child, brother, lover—it's just important that they *meet* and learn from the meeting—*even if what you learn is to say goodbye!*

So there are certain people we meet so we can break our patterns, not repeat them.

Then it hit me hard in the stomach. Deliah had been right about saying goodbye. I lowered my head as the tears rolled over my lids and down my face. I was crying partly with the relief that finally I knew how to break the patterns and I wouldn't have to go through this repeated pain—or even be killed again—but I was also sobbing because as bad as the relationship was, I was going to miss Tanya.

Now I knew that one of the reasons I had needed to find Tanya was so I would know the identity of the child with the pale green eyes.

The last thought I'd had in that life in Nazi Germany was, "I must protect this child." In my present life, I had found her again, and in this relationship I had continued to feel I had to protect her.

I also I knew that Tanya and I were born to find each other so I could learn of all our other lifetimes together and see our patterns. That was her gift to me.

Knowing *all* of this, one more thing became very clear: this time *we were born to say goodbye.*

Chapter Thirty-two

Broken Triangles

I have another duty equally sacred . . .
My duty is to myself.

—HENRIK IBSEN
A Doll's House

What do you do when you know it's over? What do you do when you have discovered a pattern that has existed over four lifetimes and want to break it?

I had the long flight from Honolulu back to California to think about it. I realized at other times, even when the weight had been more intense, the sorrow had not been as deep.

I thought of all the things we had shared, and finally, I clearly realized I wanted to break the bond.

I arrived back in Los Angeles and drove north along the coast to our apartment where our lives were so tormented. I wasn't afraid of her anymore, I wasn't even sure I'd ever realized just how *much* I'd been afraid of her all those years or even what it had been about her that made me so afraid. Now I could see that I'd always been afraid—afraid she would leave me, afraid she would kill me, afraid the patterns I craved only because they were familiar would end. Now, if I was afraid of anything, it was that the tortured, familiar patterns would *not* end.

We had to say goodbye. It didn't matter how much I loved her; it didn't matter that I died in the last life thinking I had to protect her, and then was born into this life remembering only that same thought. Now it was over, and I finally knew that this time we were born to say goodbye.

My pulse pounded, my head throbbed, and I hardly noticed that my back—which always ached where the bruise had appeared so many years ago where I now knew the rifle butt had hit me—was not aching.

I had no idea how she'd react. I realized I never knew how she'd react to *anything* I ever did or said. I was tired of chaos and pathos and triangles. I had waited for ten years for stability in our relationship, but the stability had never come! Now I felt a new life surging within *me*. I was beginning to discover my soul and to know that something inside me wanted to live and love and create beauty. I had finally seen the patterns that had been limiting me, but for my soul to grow, I had to break them.

First I called Pepper. "Pepper," I said, "you've been saying you know how we could work it all out. Well, I'm inviting you to breakfast to discuss it."

"Oh, wonderful," she said, "come to my place."

Then I called Tanya at the office. "Tanya, Pepper has invited me to breakfast at her place, and I'm inviting you. I want all of us to talk."

She was silent. Finally, she replied "I can't talk at work—you know that."

"Yes, I know that—I've always known that. But I don't see you at the apartment anymore so now I'm telling you the meeting you've always wanted can happen at Pepper's place at 9:00 tomorrow morning."

I went to the balcony and watched the sun set over the water, knowing it would be the last one I would see from that apartment.

Tanya came home late. We never spoke, but I knew she'd be there tomorrow.

The next morning Tanya sat at the table holding her coffee, mixing her cream and sugar into the black mass.

I walked back into my bedroom to collect my thoughts. Was I ready? Was I ready for this moment that would be the culmination of not one, not two, not three, but *four* lifetimes." I sighed and took a deep breath. I knew it was the breath that would sustain me and help me take this step that would affect the rest of my life.

I heard the front door open and close. Tanya had left for our meeting at Pepper's home. I waited a few moments until I knew she would be down the elevator and out of the lobby and then I walked to the door. I thought of the guides Deliah had spoken about, and I said out loud, "Be with me now, give me the strength."

I left the apartment and walked to my car. It was a short drive to Pepper's place. I would arrive only a few minutes late, but I didn't want to walk through the door at the same time as Tanya did.

When I got to Pepper's building, I parked along the street. I wanted to be as far away from Tanya's car as I could. I rode the elevator up to Pepper's apartment, approached her door, and rang the bell.

As Pepper opened the door to let me in, I noticed she looked different than I had remembered her. She had tried to dress very carefully for this momentous occasion; however the lace collar looked out of place with her red silk tie, as if she was still confused about whether to dress like a man or a woman.

"Oh Marilyn, how good to see you. I'm so glad we're having this meeting. It's long overdue."

She was trying to be all bubbly and polite, but it didn't feel genuine to me. I wasn't sure I could believe anything she said anymore, but I was still glad I was there.

"I have coffee ready, and some donuts. I think this is a special occasion. We're finally going to work out how the three of us can live together." Pepper rattled on, but I only nodded. I knew she had no idea why I was really there.

We sat down, each in a different corner of the room, forming a perfect triangle, Yes, I thought, *another triangle!*

Finally, I turned to Pepper and said, "You've always said there was a way to work this all out. What have you come up with?"

"Well, I'm working on it. I haven't really found it yet, but I know I will," Pepper replied, lifting her coffee in a cup that had a naked woman painted on the side of it.

Her answer took me by surprise. I'd really believed she had something in mind, but now I knew she had never intended to find a way.

I looked at her and I knew why she looked different. Her heavy makeup did not totally cover the fresh pink scars from her most recent facelift. Her lipstick stretched out beyond her thin lip line.

Then I looked at Tanya. "Well, Tanya, what have you come up with?"

Her voice went into a very high pitch, as it always did when she was nervous, "I'm waiting for the two of you to come up with something."

I paused a long while. I felt like letting the ridiculousness of this whole scene drain from my body as I knew all hope, all sensibility, all true reality had been drained from me over the many months of this triangle. I waited until I felt the surge of some sanity and strength within my body, within *me*.

I looked first at Pepper, then at Tanya, and fixed my eyes steadily at her pale green eyes as I knew I'd done once before during the Inquisition. Now I knew I was taking back my power. This time there was no hot poker in front of my eyes.

I let a few moments pass before I spoke. "Pepper, you've had no answer. Tanya, you have no answer. Well *I* do, and I've thought about it for a long time. I have something I want to say to you both." I paused, searching for the best way to express the thoughts I'd worked on all night. "I think there's something the two of *you* need to work out karmically."

"No, no!" Tanya was already shaking her head and waving her arms. "No! No!"

I knew she didn't believe in reincarnation nor could I explain it to her in any way she'd listen.

"Stop, Tanya. Let me finish!" I interrupted her as she had me. "I think there's something the two of you must work out karmically. You may not believe it, but I *know* it's true. What I want to say and I will only say it *once*." (I knew that's all I was able to handle.) "What I want to say is—*I give you my blessing.*"

I saw the smile cross Pepper's face as if in victory. I knew she thought she'd won. Then I faced Tanya. I saw that childlike fear— the child I'd seen shivering at the ditch in the woods in Nazi Germany. I saw the childlike, animal fear, but I continued anyway. I continued because I was breaking the need to protect her. I had seen the patterns and knew I no longer wanted to be bound by them.

For a moment, I thought of looking away. It would've been easier that way, but then I realized I needed to do this for *me* and I stared intently back at her just as I had done at the Inquisition, only this time there would be no black, and no death. There was only going to be the *truth!*

"Yes, I give you my blessing and I know what I must do." I stood up, having taken the first step in breaking the triangle, and started walking toward the door.

I turned only briefly to see the smile on Pepper's face broaden. She was sure she had won. I saw the fear in Tanya's pale green eyes as I said, "I'm leaving, I'm walking. It's finally *over!*"

Tanya started screaming, "No, no! Marilyn, please *don't!* You can't leave me—please, please, you're my *family!*"

No, I thought, I'm not your family—I'm just what's familiar to you.

I knew there was no turning back. I kept walking. I knew who *she* was. *Now I needed to find out who I was.*

I walked closer to the door. Tanya started after me—the triangle was now totally falling apart.

As I walked through the door, I murmured, ". . . born to say goodbye." Over and over I said, "born to say goodbye," as I walked to the elevator . . . "born to say goodbye, born to say goodbye," louder and louder in my head so I couldn't hear Tanya's screams.

PART III

The Integration

UP FROM EDEN

An ominous shadow of things past,
lives that might have been,
dreams dreamt yet not manifest.
Till in the whirlpool of evolution
a claw/foot takes shape.

Rising, swirling, expanding,
to emerge above the matter world.
A cry is heard,
      the sign of life at all births.

The cry of a soul finding meaning and
breathing the first breath of knowing
      its place in the universe.

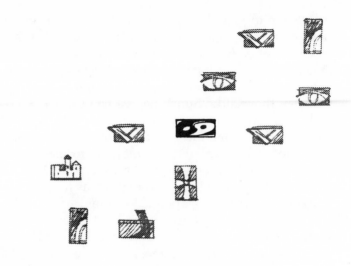

An Interlude as Home

... the darkest cloud will break ...

—HELEN KELLER
The Story of Her Life

1991, *SEDONA, ARIZONA*

It was nearly sunset as we rounded the corner and I caught sight of the majestic red rocks. Tall and regal like sentinels of another time, their vibrations reach out to touch thousands as they pass through Sedona. A handful of people stay each year. I was one of them.

When I left California, I took nothing except a suitcase, my wounded feelings, and battered memories. My paintings were already in storage. I wanted nothing else from my life with Tanya. It was as if I took even a spoon, it would contaminate me.

I felt as if I was running for my life—as I had from Madison.

I had no idea then how wounded I really was. The old patterns were broken, new ones hadn't yet formed, and, like the turtle who has shed its old shell and not yet formed its new one, I was raw, weak, and vulnerable.

For years I'd lived in silence, never telling anyone what was going on in the infrastructure of our relationship. Now I realized that the silence had isolated me and kept me from friends who could have told me my world with Tanya was not real, but madness.

I began to pick through the rubble of my bruised, battered emotions to see if I could find any sense of who I was.

Once again, Julie and Scott were there for me. They'd moved to Sun Lakes, a new community developing south of Phoenix. They gave me hours of their time to explore tender, painful memories. One day they said, "Sunshine, we want to show you Sedona."

It was while riding with them that we rounded the corner at sunset and the gigantic rock sentinels spoke to me.

Maybe it was because the majestic formations reminded me of how I felt—like a soul frozen in time—but I knew immediately I wanted to stay in Sedona, and that it was here that I would heal and integrate all that had happened to me.

Within hours I found a wonderful, dark-but-loved little home with a fountain in the front. Three weeks later the legal papers were completed and it was all mine. I also bought the TV and all the tools that went with the house.

I began at once remodeling the home that would be my sanctuary. With the TV, I preserved what sanity I had retained by watching mindless programs and going into denial when the pain became too intense.

I wanted a wall a day to tumble. I lifted ceilings, I opened and arched doorways, and I even took an axe to the center support beams, rounding them to be like pillars. With my bare hands, and to the sounds of Gregorian chant, I stuccoed walls so that more and more, the home took on the appearance of the monastery I'd seen at Assisi; more and more it became my sanctuary. I felt that it was a living being and my latest work of art. I assured the house that the makeover would only hurt for a short while and then it would be beautiful.

Nearing the end of the remodeling, I called a contractor and had him build a huge studio on the back of the house—all in glass. I landscaped the entire yard into a sculpture garden.

Six-, eight-, ten-foot canvases started parading through my studio. Where the remodeling had ended, the painting began. I painted scenes of arches and paths. Scenes from the Europe I loved. I formed them with the light and shadow I'd learned from the Impressionists. I wove colors back and forth over shimmering water and floating lily pads. I formed them into perfect patterns as if they were holograms that suggested the unending, perfect patterns of the Universe.

I started placing my work in galleries across the nation.

Painting became my life.

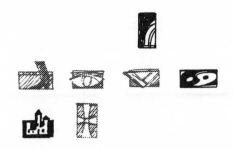

Chapter Thirty-three

A Search for Truth

You gain strength, courage and confidence by every experience
in which you really stop to look fear in the face.
—ELEANOR ROOSEVELT
You Learn by Living

It was very difficult for me to break the pattern of silence that Tanya had insisted upon for years.

Someone had given me Melody Beattie's book, *Co-Dependent No More,* which explained how some people give up their lives and start living through another and how it's possible to break this behavior. Only five pages into the book I saw myself. I had given over my power to Tanya and had entered into an agreement that she was once again the Queen.

The truly dysfunctional nature of our relationship tumbled down around me as had the walls of the house I'd remodeled. I knew that like the house, whose old structure had to be broken down to make it a sanctuary, my old personality had to shatter in order to form a healthy self.

Tanya had insisted that I never tell anyone about her affairs and the triangles she always created, but now I knew that part of my healing was talking about them and the sickness of her rules—and my acceptance of them. I knew I had to reclaim myself, the self that had been violated by behavior that was foreign to me.

It was a long journey back. Often I would call Deliah in Honolulu for my spiritual reality check, or for a more down-to-earth reality check, I would jump in my car and drive to Los Angeles where my friend Trevor lived.

Trevor was mid-height, though that was the only thing about him that was mid-anything. Everything else was strong in one way or the other. He was very dark and very sensitive, and was never afraid of the truth, for himself or someone else.

We had met at a party that Tanya and I attended in Honolulu many years before. I'd heard him telling someone off after they'd made an anti-Semitic remark and I'd instantly liked him. After that, Tanya and I often saw him at parties.

Though Trevor was twenty years younger than I, we usually closed all age gaps in our private discussions.

I had been there for Trevor after a hard breakup, and when he heard about Tanya and me, he called. He had moved to Los Angeles to heal his broken heart and start a new life, just as I had moved to Sedona.

I was visiting him in Los Angeles, and we were seated at a table at his private club when I told him details about my breakup with Tanya.

"Well, Pepper's loaded," he'd said. "It's clear she's after her money, and now we know she was just after you for your money!"

His statement made me furious. My fingers gripped under the edge of the table.

"How dare you say that about someone I've loved!" I was about to flip the table over in anger when I looked around, realized I was at his elegant private club, and instead, I just lifted my fist above the table and banged it down, hard. Then I slid back my chair, rose abruptly, and walked away. Once outside, I broke down and wept. Was he telling the truth?

It would have been easier to think Tanya had left me for someone who had more money, but I really didn't want to believe that of her. I still cared about her. But I had a motto I tried to live by: *Do not step on someone else's karma.*

The next time I talked with him, Trevor was unrelenting.

"But, she was my friend. She was with me for over ten years. I thought we were soul mates."

"She was *never* your friend, let alone your soul mate." His eyes narrowed as he went on. "She spoke behind your back all the time. You would begin one of your stories and she would be sitting there behind you, rolling her eyes upward, as if questioning your credibility. That's no friend!"

Trevor went on relentlessly. "You unrealistically put her on a pedestal," he said, and then he would begin to knock one part of my story after the other about how good she'd been to me.

He knocked at the pedestal with bits of information about her that I didn't even know until I finally wondered if I knew her at all. Every section, every part of the pedestal I had placed her on, got chipped away and the image I'd so falsely created of my soul mate, my savior, lay like shattered glass at my feet. It wasn't clear to me if it was her actual personality that splintered and fragmented, or if it was the image of her that I'd created.

I don't think Trevor ever did believe me when I told him about my past lives, but that didn't matter. What he was showing me was the truth, which was something I hadn't allowed into my life. I had created a false image of Tanya. Now, the stark truth was before me and I had to face the realities that I had created as well as the realities of my past lives. I had to admit that I had *given* my power away, and then that I must *take* it back. To heal, I had to face my demons and begin telling the truth. And I was fortunate: through the reflections in Trevor's eyes, and Deliah's, I began to see myself and like myself.

The test of how well I was doing in facing the truth was soon to come.

One day I received an anonymous letter, complete with daggers drawn with blood dripping from them. Its author, in order to disguise the handwriting, wrote in a very primitive, child-like scrawl. The message was chilling: "Cease and desist talking—OR ELSE! No one wants to hear you!"

The letter was postmarked from Bisbee, a small town in Southern Arizona that was a couple of hundred miles from Sedona. I knew no one from there.

The letter, with its dagger and threats, frightened me and sent my mind, already so bruised, down endless passageways of possibilities where dangers were waiting. I started slipping into old patterns.

I thought of Madison and his sick mind—sending strange men to find me so long ago in the streets of Minneapolis. I thought of Queens pushing me from turrets and hot pokers coming at my eyes. Could I ever really escape?

The letter had been waiting for me when I'd returned from a trip to Colorado; I'd just placed my paintings in galleries in Aspen and Vail.

I had entered the house and was sitting at my desk. Somehow the energies of my sanctuary now felt different, as if the peacefulness had been violated and the soft auric field of blue had been shattered into murky brown.

I called Rachel, a friend of mine who was very psychic, and asked her to come over. I explained to her that I didn't know what was wrong, but since I had returned from a trip somehow my house felt different. As she entered the door she drew a quick, startled breath.

"Someone has been here," she said. "Two people were here while you were gone." She scurried from room to room, holding her hands in front of her as if to test for what could be felt but not seen.

Upon entering each room, she said, "Two women have been here—they have invaded your space." Then she began to describe them. "One a little taller than the other. One much older. One grey hair—the other soft brown."

She continued on, perfectly describing Tanya and Pepper. I wanted to deny that they could have done this. I wanted to believe I was making the whole thing up in my mind, but there was the possibility it was true. I knew that Tanya and Pepper could have broken in, that the insanity was still around me and that *they may have violated my sanctuary.*

Rachel stopped in front of a rosewood chair, a beautiful antiqué replica of a royal chair from a Chinese dynasty. It was quite out of place with my contemporary furniture. It had been one of Tanya's favorites and she had unexpectedly sent it to me as her peace offering: "Can't we be friends now?" she asked in the note that had come with it. I'd always felt uneasy with the chair and now I realized that I shouldn't have kept it at all.

"Get rid of it—today, if you can. Its energy is definitely negative— it's almost as if it's spying on you! It has the same energy as one of the women who's been in your house."

Many people come to Sedona for its heightened spiritual energy and for growth. This path does not allow you to stay in denial long. I'd already been in denial far too long and had nearly broken the time barrier on long-term "nonbelief".

I went to the desk and brought out the threatening letter with the daggers drawn on it and placed it in Rachel's hand. She drew her hand back as if it had just touched a hot flame. The letter fell to the floor. As I bent to pick it up I noticed, for the first time, the little round circles that formed the dots over the "i's"—little round circles like Tanya used to draw over her "i's" when her guard was down and what I called her "evil child" came out. Of course, Tanya had sent the letter and I saw how right Trevor had been all along.

I let the connecting links join in my mind: Tanya and Pepper must have driven through here on the way to Bisbee. It was all beginning to make sense. I'd remembered Pepper had a niece in Bisbee. They must have gone to visit her, driven through here, and when I wasn't home, they came in anyway.

My mind continued connecting one piece of the chain to the next. Breaking in wouldn't have been difficult for Tanya; she'd always felt she could read my mail and that she had the right to enter wherever she wished, just like the Queen! So after leaving here they drove on to Bisbee and mailed the letter from there. With the final link in the chain, it was clear to me what had happened and I *didn't* like it.

That day I gave the chair away and called to have my house formally blessed.

At first I thought Tanya and I could settle our joint ownership of the Santa Alicia apartment and some other property amicably, but it was soon apparent that she did not want to let go of me *or* the property. I realized then that she never wanted to let go of anything. I thought back to the story she'd told me about her father and how he'd abandoned her.

"I swear," Tanya had yelled, "I'll *never* let anyone leave me again!"

And it was clear: Tanya felt I had left her, that I had abandoned her.

After a year in which we made no progress toward a settlement, I hired a lawyer. My lifelong pattern of powerlessness was exposed in the white sweat I felt at sitting before the second lawyer I'd ever had to hire.

The lawyer told me I must be firm, that I might have to expose the relationship for what it was—two woman in a love relationship— if I was to continue on with my self-esteem. If I was to continue on with *anything*.

It became clearer and clearer to me that Tanya was afraid of her dark side, and the thought that she would be exposed before the world would send her into a rage.

The rage was not long in coming. She'd received my attorney's letter, and called, screaming into the phone, "How *dare* you! How dare you threaten me this way—you know we can work this out between us."

"No," I said, "no, I don't know that." I'd rehearsed it over and over in my mind, telling myself to remain calm and not *give* my power away, *not* let her drive me into giving in and telling her just to take it all—and *not* let her drive me back into a past pattern or near to the edge of the turret.

Tanya had wanted us to remain friends and to talk often. At first I had wanted that also, still missing her and thinking it was the mature thing to do, but soon I realized she didn't want to let go at all.

"No," I said firmly, "we can't talk anymore. You must get a lawyer and it will be settled between the lawyers—or in a courtroom."

I hung up, shaking, but it was the first conversation with Tanya in a very long time in which I didn't feel battered.

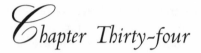

One Last Look

... our power is there for the taking. It is free, inherent in nature.
By the simplest gesture, we can reclaim it ...
                                        —MARILYN FERGUSON
                                        The Aquarian Conspiracy

Snowflakes flew around my head. I had no scarf. I had no boots.

My small slipper-like shoes hardly covered my feet as I pressed on for block after block and the flurries became thicker.

I was having an art show in Chicago. I'd seen the sun reflecting off the high-rise across the street when I'd gone to the door of the hotel where I was staying, and decided it was a lovely day to go for a walk. It was my day off from the show and it looked so warm. I'd started toward the old haunts I'd known so many years ago, but it began to turn cold and now it was snowing.

I didn't know the cold would come, nor did I know it would expose the places deep inside me that I'd frozen into denial so many years before.

As I walked, the snow became deeper around my feet, and I

remembered the time when I was running barefoot through the streets of Germany trying to escape Madison.

Here I was again in Chicago, the city where I'd met him and loved him, become pregnant by him, and then lost the chance ever to have a baby again.

I kept walking, stopping in front of each place that Madison and I had shared.

Years before, I'd devised a method that I called "clearing." It was simple and powerful. I began to use it now in front of each place that had emotional pain connected to it. I would stand there, allowing the painful memories to resurface and wash through my mind and body. I would stand there for however long it took, however many tears it took, until I'd exhausted all the pathos. Once all the pain and tears were gone, a most delightful thing would happen—good, warming memories would rush in and I knew I was cleared—healed!

Using this method I'd learned, with any place or event, most often there's been some good as well as some bad, and that frequently one goes into denial of one or the other, seeing only the bad, or seeing only the good. In my case, I didn't remember any of the good because my feelings had been frozen only in the past pain.

So once I'd cleared away the painful memories, I could begin to remember some of the good times, the fun. With this clearing, I could walk on, knowing I was free from the past and ready to move on with my life.

Tears had laced my cheeks at each place and I hardly noticed them mixing with the snowflakes as they touched my cheeks. When I had cried what seemed like a river and had done all my healing, I turned to head back to the hotel where my art show was waiting.

I passed a dark window where I could see only a reflection of what was passing on the street. I remembered it was the bar where Madison and I had met, The Existential Mystic. My eyes traced along the windows and up to the sign above the door. I read, The Cross-Eyed Frog and laughed. Yes, the mystic had probably been kissed by a Queen and turned into a frog.

I walked through the door. It took several moments for my eyes to adjust to the darkness. Inside, nothing had changed. The long wooden bar that stretched the entire length of the room was still there, its surface laced with thousands of initials that had been carved into it over the years. The varnish had turned dark from all the smoke that had drifted over it and all the greasy hands that had clutched it.

I went to the far end of the bar, pulled back the stool, and ordered a glass of white wine as I sat down. What if Madison should walk in? Was I still afraid of him? I knew this was my chance to handle any fears I had left. I could either heal the wounds now, or I would spend the rest of my life not knowing whether I thought I had to run and hide. I sat for moments before I felt a calm descend over me, a calm that told me I was no longer afraid of him.

I took a deep sip of my wine and taking a long-shot, I asked the bartender if he knew a Madison Cooper.

His "Yes" took me by surprise. He took delight in the shock he'd seen in my eyes and went on, "He comes in once in a while, always gets drunk—probably was his prison time that did him in."

"Prison time?" I didn't even try to disguise my shock.

"Ya. It was his fifth or sixth wife and he used her for bow and arrow practice. He tied her at the end of the hall. Don't know if it killed her, but it made pretty big headlines some years back."

Shuddering, I finished my wine and turned to go.

The bartender, still enjoying my frown, yelled after me, "I've always wondered if he beat any of his other wives."

I was walking through the door as I said in a low, raw, raspy voice, "He did."

Chapter Thirty-five

Healing Goodbyes

In the face of Men and Women I see God, and in my own
face in the glass . . .

—WALT WHITMAN
Leaves of Grass

It was a long drive back to Minnesota. I turned to Apollo, who was sitting on the seat next to me in his Gucci bag, and said. "Toto, do you think we'll ever get out of Kansas?" He loved to travel and watch the scenery go by, but most of all he loved the hamburgers I would buy him at McDonald's.

I knew that if I was ever to heal, not only did I have to see the patterns of my past lives, but I had to get in touch with the patterns of this lifetime since both were involved in my choosing such disastrous relationships.

It had been my intention to search for my patterns, beginning with my parents, but when I arrived in Minnesota, I found that my father needed a lot of attention. He was in great pain most of the time. His emphysema had progressed to the point that his breathing was always labored. The medication he'd been taking caused his bones to become brittle and his spine had shrunk.

Usually it was my mother and I who would talk. We had grown

much closer since I'd torn down my self-imposed walls and had risked sharing intimate parts of myself. She had also begun to share some of her dreams with me, dreams she expressed through her poetry and writings.

This time, it was Dad who wanted to talk. He drew me close to him on the couch and all the years of separation melted. It was as if after all his years of silence, he was trying to find his voice.

"Marilyn, I know I've never told you, or anyone, about my father, but he was a good man." I took Dad's hand and began to rub it gently as he went on. "Maybe he should never have been a farmer. He was a deep man, a thinker, like you. He loved to read poetry and Shakespeare. Farming seemed to be so hard for him."

"Dad, I had no idea he was like that. I wish I had known him."

"Oh, Marilyn, it was so hard when he died. I was just a kid, only twelve years old, and finding him in the pasture like that—after he'd taken poison. I thought I'd never get over it. I *miss* him so much!"

We both sat there as the tears began to stream down our faces. It was only the second time I'd ever seen my father cry. The first was the time he and Mom had told us about Grandpa's suicide.

"I miss my little sister, too," he continued. "She and I were such good friends. We always played together. I was two years older and I always tried to protect her. Then one day, when she was five, she got this high fever and the folks put her to bed. Within a couple days she was dead. I don't know what it was—I don't even know if *they* knew what it was. They just didn't talk about it or tell me anything. All I remember was that there was always this silence around the house, and so I just kept waiting for it to be my turn to get a fever and die."

I took Dad into my arms and rocked his frail, bent body very gently back and forth so I wouldn't hurt his brittle spine. After some time he drew back from me so he could speak.

Will I see them again?" he asked. "Will I see my father? Do you believe I'll see my little sister?" His eyes were searching into mine. "Do you believe in the Tunnel of Light?"

Years before, I'd attended a workshop on self-healing and on processing the death experience given by Dr. Elisabeth Kübler-Ross. I'd originally gone to it because I was going to do a portrait of her. She'd seen a portrait I'd done of the Prime Minister of Israel, Golda Meir.

"If you can make Golda look that good," she'd said, "you can paint me!"

Within only ten minutes of the start of the workshop, I knew I was there for more than a portrait. I was there for my own healing and for my journey home . . . my journey back to believing.

While I was painting the portrait, we became friends. Since she had admired Golda's portrait so much, I thought I'd paint her in a similar fashion.

I had begun a series of what I called "The Greats," all portraits of people whom I felt had been exceptional, and had painted Golda in three images on the canvas to represent the three sides of this complex world leader. The image on the right showed her as the statesperson, the center as the deep thinker, and the largest image to the left was the soft, vulnerable Grandma Golda.

So I felt the complexity of Dr. Elisabeth Kübler-Ross could only be captured as I'd painted Golda—in three images. Well, her guides—her "spooks," as she calls them—had a different thought in mind.

Her guides appeared to me blazoned across my windshield, just as Mrs. Wong's portrait had appeared years before, and said—*one* Image—but a saintly one—and dressed that way! Now, anyone who knows Elisabeth, knows she prefers shorts and Birkenstocks. Well, the guides gave me the image of her in a gown, a long gown with pointed sleeves down to her wrists. Every detail was there from the open collar to a color scheme I couldn't imagine, orange and purple trim with the same color in the shadows over a basic beige (later I was to discover it was this color combination that allowed my paintings to have an inner glow so that they had a spiritual radiance about them). I tried to argue with her guides, even tried to have my guides intercede with hers, but they only confirmed what her "spooks" said. And then to cap it all off, her guides told me I was to give a faint hint of one of them over her left shoulder.

No one had ever seen Elisabeth dressed the way I was portraying her. So with great trepidation, I called her to tell her that her portrait was finished.

"I'm coming to Honolulu soon," Elisabeth said. "I can't wait to see if I look as good as Golda."

Now I was even more concerned of the liberties her "spooks" had taken with her portrait.

Elisabeth entered the room, we hugged, then she immediately asked to see *her Golda*. My hand shook slightly as I unveiled the painting. She stood back and stared at it, then walked farther back and stared again before reaching into her purse. She withdrew an old, used envelope that had a drawing on its fold side, and handed it to me.

"On the plane over here, I decided I should dress up more when I give my speeches on death and dying," Elisabeth said, still staring at her portrait. "So I drew this sketch of a gown I was going to have made."

Her sketch on the envelope was of a long gown. It had an open collar and pointed sleeves that reached to the wrists. It perfectly matched the gown her spooks had told me to paint on her portrait. All the details were there just as I had painted them.

"Okay, okay, so you were right!" I said out loud to her guides.

We hugged again and then sat down while I told her the story of how her portrait came to be so different from what either of us had expected it to be.

During our friendship and from her workshop, I learned not only about healing, but about the Tunnel of Light and how loved ones would always be at the end of the tunnel waiting to guide us home to the Light.

"Marilyn, will I see them again? Do you believe in the Tunnel of Light?" Dad asked me even more urgently.

"Yes, Dad, I *do* believe in the Tunnel of Light."

Because of Elisabeth, and my experiences since knowing her, I could answer honestly, "And, you *will* see your father and your little sister again. They'll be waiting for you." His frail shoulders relaxed as his breathing became more steady.

On the first day in Minnesota I had talked to Dad's doctor. She'd assured me it would be weeks, perhaps months, before it was Dad's time. "His heart is still strong," she had said.

Dad was searching through his own beliefs about dying. I could see that he'd always thought that dying was a sin, that it was a sin to leave your children the way his father had left him.

On the fourth night of my visit, I was at my brother's when the phone rang. It was my mother. "Your father's dying. Please come right away!"

Even though the doctor had said that it wasn't his time, it was happening.

I walked into the room. Never had Mom been so firm. "Your father is ready to go. We've discussed it. He needs to hear you tell him it's all right."

I thought back to the three days of talks he and I had about the

Light, and I knew he'd come to the end of his search. I took him in my arms.

Remembering all the lessons I'd learned from Dr. Kübler-Ross about being with someone in their last precious moments, I began to stroke his head gently.

"You have been a good father and a good husband, Dad," I said softly. "If you're ready, it's okay to go to the Light."

I pulled my hand gently across his brow as I said, "I love you."

From deep in his throat came a small, purposeful voice, "I love you."

His eyes focused on Mom. She'd drawn her chair closer and was now only three feet away. There was a deep rattling in his chest, almost drowning out his words as he said to her, "Ma, I love you."

A soft smile crossed his face. His head fell onto my shoulder. I knew he was now experiencing the peacefulness I'd experienced when I had died in the other lifetimes.

Later, Mom was to share with me how she saw his angel lift his soul from his body.

I spent the next few days walking the places I used to go as a child. It seemed that so many of them were places I had gone to hide. What was I always hiding from?

Then I remembered how often, as a child, I had heard my father's angry voice and how it frightened me. My mother was always trying to protect him from his own feelings, especially his feelings about his father's suicide and being abandoned.

Madison's father had also abandoned *him* and Madison was always angry. Is that why I chose him? Tanya's father had also abandoned her and her mother. Is that why she had such anger? Then, as if waking up, I suddenly made a connection for the first time: I had married a man who had the same birthday as my father and I began to make all the connections between abandonment, fear, and anger.

A deep and compelling feeling of compassion came over me for the child, Madison, and for the child, Tanya. They'd both been abandoned by their fathers and left to find any way they could to stifle their hurt.

I saw the connection between their hurt and anger and their need to control more and more of their world and the people around them so they could try to feel powerful or *safe*. And then I saw *my* connection with powerlessness and *my* need to be controlled by angry, hurtful people.

I stopped walking and sat down on a tree stump. I knew I was in the pasture where Dad had gone to get the cows and had found his father lying dead. I wept for the small, lost child my father must have been at that moment. I wept for the small, lost child I had been so much of my life.

Now I could see that all of us—my brothers, Mom, and I—had always tried to protect Dad from his feelings.

So there I sat, thinking: I was killed in one lifetime trying to protect someone in Nazi Germany, then born into a family that was always protecting someone from their feelings. No wonder I assumed that pattern with Madison and with Tanya. I had been carefully trained. No wonder it was so difficult to walk away from Tanya. No wonder I'd felt like I'd abandoned her when I left—I was breaking a pattern of many lifetimes.

Later, when it was time to go home, I said goodbye to my kid brother, Dustin. We had shared our tears and some memories. We discussed one last one.

"So, Dustin, that's why it was so hard for Dad to face death. He thought that when you die you abandon the ones you love. That's what Dad felt had happened when Grandpa committed suicide.

"I had to have been nineteen and you fifteen when we first heard about it," I went on. "I think someone close to Dad had died and he felt so bad about the death, it triggered him into thinking about killing himself. He decided not to do it, then promised us he would never take his own life and leave us like his father had left him. That's the first time we'd even heard about it, only Dad was crying so much he couldn't talk, and Mom had to tell us."

"No," Dustin said, a puzzled look crossing his face, "no, that's not how I remember it. I don't remember anyone dying—I remember going to the storeroom that was on the side of the house. I was going to clean it out. I don't think anyone had touched it for years. I found this old smelly bottle of who knows what and was carrying it out of the shed when Dad caught sight of me with *that bottle.* He tore into me. He yelled. He fumed. I finally just walked away from him. I was quite a distance away when I heard his ranting turn into sobs."

Dustin and I stared at each other in silence. We both knew what Dustin had found that day. It was the bottle of poison my grandfather had used so many years before and that's what had *exposed Dad's feelings,* and why his ranting had turned to tears.

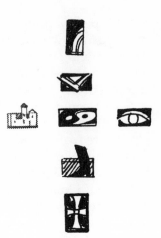

Chapter Thirty-six

Healing Memories

It is one thing to talk about ... the meaning of life, but such ...
can't compare to the difficulty of making sense of your life.
—ELISABETH KÜBLER-ROSS
The Wheel of Life

As my strength grew, so did the size of my canvases.

I had to hire an assistant to handle varnishing, packing, and shipping to all the galleries that now carried my work, and a manager to oversee all the things I couldn't personally keep up with.

My subject matter continued to be paths, doorways, and bridges. They all led to hope and light. As my paintings became lighter, so did my life, and I even began to paint the angels I felt around me.

I'd had a vision of a scene with two people standing along the shore, staring hopefully into the dawning horizon and had captured it in a large painting. After its publication in a national magazine, I got a synchronistic phone call from Nina L. Diamond, a writer in Florida, who'd had the same vision.

"I've been interviewing Brian Weiss for a number of articles, including one for *Omni* magazine, and during our first interview, I had him hypnotize me for a past-life regression. Instead of a past life, I saw a 'between lives' series of scenes. I saw the vision of the couple in your painting—*a full year before I ever saw your painting published.* In fact, the woman is *me*," Nina said excitedly.

"How ironic," I said. "I've just finished reading *Through Time Into Healing,* one of Brian Weiss's books about reincarnation. I've even been using some of his methods to get in touch with more information from my past lives. This has to be more than a coincidence!"

"Well, I want to do an article on your work, too," she said. "I'll call you in a couple days."

On the second call from Nina she mentioned she'd again been in touch with Dr. Brian Weiss and that they had subsequently discussed my painting.

"Brian would like to meet you," she said. "Do you ever come to Florida? We could do your interview and I could introduce you to him."

I was thrilled by this revelation and by the thought of meeting Dr. Brian Weiss. I felt I could gain a great deal more knowledge from him about the search into past lives. And in light of these coincidences, I felt it was fated that I was to meet Dr. Weiss, just as I'd learned it was fated that I would visit so many of the places in Europe where I'd had past lives.

I arranged to fly to Florida almost immediately. Nina and I had an instant rapport and after spending a couple of days on the interview, she called Dr. Weiss. Along with her writing, Nina composed music, and she arranged for Dr. Weiss and me to meet during her recording of some piano music.

The soft, melodious music was drifting into the room where Dr. Weiss and I had gone to talk.

"Tell me about yourself," Dr. Weiss said in a tone that matched the gentleness of Nina's music.

"My paintings are my words," I said softly. "They are filled with spiritual light, like my life. I truly feel happiness and the Light all around me."

Dr. Weiss listened carefully, occasionally responding in his soft, attentive voice. Then he would nod and encourage me to continue.

He seemed so sensitive and complex, I wanted to be interviewing him as I so often had done for the subjects of my portraits. I began asking him about himself and his work. I'd had so many experiences searching into my own past lives that it was a golden treasure to be talking to a renowned psychiatrist who did past-life regressions.

"Would you like a regression?" he asked.

When I searched into past lives prior to reading Dr. Weiss's book, *Through Time Into Healing,* it had all been on my own. But after reading his book, I followed his suggestion: I taped my own voice, listened to it, and then could go into a self-hypnotic state. In this state I received many pieces to the puzzle and unfolding of my karmic patterns. Still, I'd never been professionally regressed. His suggestion sent my mind racing between fear and curiosity.

"I'd love it," I finally answered, curiosity winning out.

Dr. Weiss suggested a time for me to meet him at his office. The next day, with great anticipation, I drove to his South Miami office. I was sure I would get in touch even more profoundly with my spiritual path and purpose.

He ushered me into an inner room and suggested I sit down in its deep, reclining leather chair.

"Have you ever been hypnotized before?" Brian asked almost hypnotically.

"No," I said, "I've only been using the method in your book and listening to a tape of my own voice so I could go into a self-hypnotic state."

"Has it worked well for you?"

"Yes, I can go into it quite deeply and I've been able to get many answers to the questions I've had regarding my past-life patterns."

"Good, we'll see if we can go further into your exploration today." His voice seemed to get even softer and I felt him begin to speak in a purposeful rhythm. "I will hypnotize you and suggest you go back to another time. You can go back as far as you'd like. Later you can share about it if you wish."

His voice sounded muffled and its cadence began to be matched by my breathing as I descended into another time—or a place *in between lives.*

Prior to this, all the searching I'd done into the spiritual had led me to find a glorious primrose path. Angels, light beings, and angelic guides danced through my life and across my canvases. Little was I prepared for what was to happen when Dr. Weiss led me into a regression.

I heard the last of his voice as I totally slipped under. I hoped I would say something profound about whatever came up for me.

Well, I hit the BLACK. I mean, THE BLACK! There was no sound. There was no light. There was nothing!! And I could make no sound, I couldn't even grunt—so I knew I was *not* in a dark cave as a cavewoman—I was in the void. And when I came out, I was furious—my dancing with the angels and light beings was gone. I had seen THE BLACK.

I could not tell him what had happened to me—I didn't know yet. I only knew I felt different *and I wasn't happy about it.*

I thanked Dr. Weiss for his time and the regression, but inside I felt strange—as if a whole new, yet perhaps dark, part of me was awakening.

Thus began the true search into my spiritual depths. This regression with Dr. Weiss *had been* profound—it led me into a whole new quest on my journey home. I had been kicked into the next phase of my growth, the search for my shadow side. It had become time for me to do the integration of the dark and the light of my soul.

On my return to Sedona, I would daily go into a quiet space and listen to the tape Dr. Weiss had given me so I could trace back into my past lifetimes.

Finally, I realized that since so much of my history had been in Europe, I needed to go there to continue my search and integration. I called Deliah in Honolulu and asked her if she'd like to take a trip to Europe. It took her only moments to say yes.

I made all the arrangements for us to spend a month there.

We started out in Paris. I always had to see Paris. It was the city where I *knew* there were angels. I walked humming through the Tuileries. I was so filled with aliveness.

Our plan was to drive from Paris into the French Bordeaux countryside, then over the Pyrenees and into Spain. My niece had been chosen to represent the United States in wheelchair basketball at the Olympics that would be held in Barcelona, and it would be fun to see her play.

I loved to read maps and as I was studying the route, I noticed we would pass only fifty miles from Lourdes. I mentioned it to Deliah and she swung off the main road toward the town we'd both heard so much about. In a grotto in Lourdes the Virgin Mary had appeared to a young girl named Bernadette. Following that, thousands went there—and still do, to see where the miracle occurred and to be healed by the waters.

As we approached Lourdes, Deliah turned the wheel over to me. She rarely liked driving into cities. I drove through the city and started up a small hill. As I neared the top, I slipped into a parking place.

All through the city, it never occurred to me to ask for directions. I exited the car and started walking. Deliah followed me, a few paces behind. I turned to look back at her, and suddenly realized I knew exactly where I was going, as if I had been there before, but in another lifetime. Deliah was smiling—she knew I'd been there.

Lourdes opened me like a flowering lotus. As I climbed down to the grotto I could barely contain my joy at walking where it was so familiar and where I knew I'd had a wonderful life. This was truly special. By now, with all my past-life searches, I knew one is rarely blessed with a flashback or a memory when it is peaceful. They are usually connected with trauma, something you need to work on or work through, but now—for once—I was being given my daisy field.

I didn't even need to close my eyes to see the sandals form on my feet, or have my white slacks change to a flowing robe that covered my body. As I ran my delicate fingers over the moist stones, I knew I had touched the stones of this grotto many lifetimes ago. Pictures formed in my mind, and soon I was a part of them:

I felt the cool water flow between my fingers, then cupped my hands so I could collect some of the healing water and place it upon the head of the woman kneeling in front of me. She lifted her face toward me and her gentle smile told me that some of her pain had vanished.

People came every day to the grotto to hear the stories I would weave about love and to feel the cool water that would so often heal their pain— both of mind and body.

A breeze wrapped my long, tan robe around my ankles, just as peace wrapped around my heart.

Only after I'd spent forty minutes with the solitude of many memories did we hear the horns and look to see a large procession of people, some ill and disabled in carts, heading toward the healing waters. As the flood of people passed by, I knew I'd just been given a miracle: a special quiet time with no people around so that I could remember that lifetime. Deliah stood beside me, smiling.

This was to be the first of several flashbacks I was destined to experience on this trip through Europe—this pilgrimage into past lives.

I was silent for a long time as we drove over the Pyrenees toward Barcelona. Lourdes had been magically, enchantingly joyous for me, as very few past memories had ever been.

Now, as I continued to try to bring back the joy and the opening in my soul that I felt at Lourdes, a foreboding of what was to come pulled in around me.

I was not aware then that holding myself open like that would make me more vulnerable to the darkness that awaited me. I had not yet learned to wrap a protection of white light around me.

During my many years of travel I had always avoided Barcelona, even when I had been in nearby Madrid. Now that I was in Barcelona, I didn't know why I'd avoided it. It was charming, beautiful, and full of art.

Deliah had found the route to a special Picasso museum. It led us past the oldest existing church in Barcelona, which had been built over the ruins of an even older one. Deliah insisted we go into the darkened church before going on to the museum.

I peered into the interior of the church through its small, wood-framed doorway. The huge interior was lit only by the rays of the sun that poured through some of its stained glass windows.

Deliah entered before me and called back, "Come here, this is important. You must come in."

I hesitated. I didn't know why. An ominous darkness seemed to be gathering about me, a darkness I had felt before. It was amassing around my eyes.

A foot-high board crossed the base of the doorway. I had to step over it as I entered. This strange foreboding feeling of darkness grew greater and heavier as I walked past one row of benches and then the next.

My legs became heavier—heavier—as if chains were wrapped around my ankles, and I could only drag my feet in shorter and shorter steps. My shoulders began to sag as my breathing labored from my chest. I reached my hand out to grab the back of a bench to keep from falling, then I slipped into a pew. I let my leaden body fall like stone-weight onto the dark wooden bench.

Warm, velvety liquid quickly formed around my eyes. Chains were clamped around my ankles. Dark leather straps around my wrists held my throbbing hands tightly against the rough arm rests of the wooden chair.

My eyes lifted from the blood red triangle at my feet being formed by the sun shining through a stained glass window. A man in a black robe was standing in front of me, his pale green eyes seething.

When they had first arrested me and brought me to this darkened chamber, I was able to hold my faith as a canopy of warmth around me. All my life I had tried to preach only love, compassion, and healing. I was a woman who had wandered for years across Spain, France, and Italy, often disguising myself as a monk so I could travel more easily. Then, as they continued to interrogate me about my beliefs and my healing abilities, the anger grew within me and my power began to retreat into my eyes.

They tormented me for days, demanding, "Do you worship the devil? What demons do you have? Has Satan given you these powers?"

Rage boiled from deep within me, rising higher and higher up my spine like a coiled snake getting ready to spring. The rage spread throughout my body and into my heart. From this I drew more power and forced it into my eyes. I glared with seething fury at the man with the pale green eyes. I could see to the depth of his weaknesses and I knew my powers were stronger.

Then they discovered I was a woman and the torture began.

The wrath was inflamed in me as the pain throbbed more and more intensely in my body.

I fought back the only way I felt I could, with my mind. My thoughts churned as all the compassion and love I'd once known was turning to fury and hatred. In my crazed delirium, I shouted, "Power, I have power—LOOK AT ME—I WILL DESTROY YOU! I will destroy you with my eyes!" My thoughts teeming with hatred, I continued, "My eyes will kill you. Just look into my eyes. I have the power of life and death over you."

My tormentor, the Inquisitor with the bloodless green eyes, would not look at me. "You coward," I taunted, "I am more powerful than you." My serpentine fury and hatred flamed higher and higher like white heat. *"I will kill you with my eyes!"*

The Inquisitor snarled as he retreated. Now I could not see him. I could only see my own rage looming before me in white heat like a hot poker. My full dark side was exposed.

Something struck the side of my head near my eyes, then started going into the sockets behind my eyes. "They're gouging my eyes out!" a voice screamed within my head. I felt the warm liquid flowing out from around my eyes and down over my cheeks. "It's my blood, my own blood. You cowards, you've taken out my eyes!" the voice in my mind screamed. "You knew I could kill you with my eyes!"

Then I felt the pain stab into my heart. The snarling, hissing snake of rage that had risen through my body began to recoil downward, letting its weakened, limp body slip into loose folds as it settled back into the base of my spine.

The dark wrapped gently around my pulsing temples, joining and blending with the warm liquid flowing down over my cheeks, then my shoulders, down through my arms, and into my throbbing hands.

Soon the gentle black became a velvet darkness and I felt peace, a peace that grew deeper and deeper as a tunnel appeared before me. A spot of light began to grow at the end of the tunnel. It was a warm light and I wanted to go toward it.

"Marilyn, Marilyn, come back, please come back. It's not your time." I heard Deliah's firm, pleading voice.

I did not want to come back. I wanted to go toward the light, the light that held more peace than I had ever felt, the Light that I knew held love.

"Marilyn, Marilyn." I heard Deliah's even more urgent voice.

In my mind I reached for the light, trying to draw nearer to it, even as I felt something pulling me backward—backward into the dark.

I felt Deliah's hands on my shoulders. She shook me gently. I let my head roll to one side so my inflamed temple could rest against the hand that she still held to my shoulder.

The warm liquid around my eyes turned from blood to tears.

Deliah braced her shoulder under my arm and lifted me from the bench of the old, Gothic-somber church in Barcelona. My legs could barely support me. I was drained and fevered.

Deliah and I didn't need to exchange words: our thoughts reached each other. I knew she had seen that this would happen to me, that we had gone to Lourdes not to find my daisy field, but to open me like a lotus flower so I could experience the light of the lifetime that had started with love and compassion but had ended in the dark of fury and hatred.

So that was it: with my dying thoughts of wanting to wield power over someone else and kill them, I had seen the dark of my own soul and had become frightened by my own darkness, my own power. So this fear actually grew into fear of myself—of who I was, *and I made myself powerless* in my next life and thus *attached myself even more firmly to the karmic wheel*, the wheel of cause and effect.

The doctor told me I had pneumonia and that the area around my heart was inflamed. "This could have killed you—you are lucky!" he said as he wrote out a prescription for antibiotics. "And now some sunshine would certainly be good for you."

"Please, Deliah, take me to Assisi," I said. "I've always loved it there—at least in my lifetime there I walked in peace and compassion."

In Assisi I took in the sunshine and did more healing.

Deliah laughed and said, "It almost looks like your home in Sedona, except for the Grecian pillars and your Roman ruin dig in your backyard." I glanced at her as she continued. "You've never gotten in touch with those lifetimes have you?"

"No," I said. "It must have all been peacefulness during those lifetimes. Other than pillars and arches and knowing I'd worked on the Parthenon, nothing has ever come up for me. Sometimes I think you're given a life of rest or at least a respite from the turmoil. Maybe Greece was my reprieve from all the pathos and I only have fond memories from that lifetime."

We left Assisi and began the journey back toward Paris. It would lead us across Switzerland, but I told Deliah I definitely did *not* want to go to Germany. "I've had all of Germany I need for two lifetimes," I said.

I had insisted we go to Lucerne in Switzerland, another city I'd always loved. Though it brought back memories of my fight with Tanya the day I'd gone to the top of the mountain, I was sure I could handle it now. Deliah reminded me that it would take us quite a bit out of our way and very close to Germany, but I insisted.

All went well in Lucerne. "See, I'm all right with it. I've done my clearing on it," I told Deliah as I showed her the covered wooden bridge that crossed the river and separated the old section of Lucerne from the new. As we were walking across the bridge, I looked up at the open window of the chalet just at the end of the walkway. I recognized it as the window I had looked out of the night Tanya and I had that terrible fight after we had come down from the mountain, the night when she hit me and I'd been knocked out— and where I'd vowed I'd *never* leave her. How strange that I should love Lucerne so much after what had happened there. But at least I had *left* her!

Driving out of Lucerne, Deliah and I headed toward the freeway. Once on the freeway, I kept cautioning Deliah, "Don't miss the turn-off to France. Don't take me to Germany." Neither of us had read about border crossings and I didn't remember that you could only cross at certain cities.

We were getting closer to the turn-off from the autobahn. The signs said, FRANCE—TWO MILES. GERMANY—AHEAD.

"France is to the left," I said. I'm sure it'll be to the left, and Germany is to the right." But as I said that, my eyes caught the sign saying FRANCE looming just to the right of us. We didn't have enough time to change lanes to exit to it. I tried to make a joke of it by saying, "F—R—A—N—C—E—" as we sped by it.

Germany lay ahead and I could feel the throbbing in my chest increase, as if fluid were again filling the cavities of my lungs.

The autobahn took us into Germany. There were no more signs to France. We had missed the border crossing and there wouldn't be another for hours. We tried changing autobahns twice, but each time we only got further and further from the border, further and further into Germany. Since we could not turn around, we now finally realized that the border crossings were only in specific cities and very far apart. We drove in silence. I dreaded knowing I was in Germany again.

Soon Deliah exited the autobahn and began to drive through the countryside. We drove through one small village after another. I stopped trying to read the map. My eyes were floating in liquid, and my breathing was becoming more and more labored.

Something about the countryside felt familiar, but I knew it was not where I had traveled as a student or lived with Madison.

Deliah drove on, only occasionally glancing at me as I coughed.

The small village we entered seemed quiet and the streets were empty. We passed a building I recognized as a school and I could see a young boy through the open window. His hand was raised. I could only wonder what question he wanted to ask the headmaster.

We passed the center of town. There was a large plaque mounted on a stone pillar. We drove by too fast for me to read it, but I knew what it would say anyway. It would list all those who had died there during the war.

We exited the town and drove by a woods. I turned to watch the trees go by, my head twisting further and further to the right until the woods was out of sight.

"That's where I died," I said to Deliah. "That's where I died during World War II. There's a long, deep ditch in the woods where woman and children . . ." I paused before going on, knowing this was the ditch I envisioned with Tanya. ". . . a *ditch where Tanya and I were shot . . . and buried!*" She nodded and we drove on in silence. Our thoughts exchanged again. I knew she'd had a vision of it before I'd even seen it.

I wondered if my name was on the plaque I'd seen back in the village. I knew that it had been no accident that we'd missed that turn in France. There are no coincidences in life.

In Europe I bumped into all the past lives I had shared with Tanya except the one in the castle. I wondered if it was because I didn't need to find that one, that I had already been in a castle during my first trip to Europe as a student, and that I had probably already handled my powerlessness in that lifetime. Now, it was how I'd made myself powerless in *this* lifetime that I had left to face.

I finally realized that my quest had never been for fame and fortune, it was always the search for my soul—to find it again and reclaim it. Little did I know it had always been hidden inside me and all I had to do was drop the old patterns of self-denial and self-abuse, just drop *all* my past patterns that were based on the karmic belief of cause and effect.

That all I had to do was—BE—BE WHO I AM!

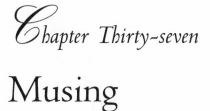

Chapter Thirty-seven

Musing

*Trust the wisdom of your soul ... that formulated your concept
of life ...*

—EMMANUEL
Emmanuel Book II, The Choice for Love

Once back in Sedona the dry air began working on the fluid caught
in my lungs, drying it, just as knowing you're where you belong can
dry the tears.

Apollo was happy to see me and jumped up on my lap. He stayed
there for hours, as if to say, "You're not going anywhere without
me ever again."

A psychic had told me that Apollo had been a little girl, a little
human girl in his last lifetime. It was the first time I'd thought of
the concept of a human becoming an animal and not the other way
around, but now as I thought of it, it seemed so right that one could
incarnate into a life where one could learn the lessons they needed
to learn.

As I stared at Apollo, I tried to picture his last lifetime as a little
girl. I looked into his eyes as they looked back at me and he appeared
to be studying my soul.

Wouldn't it be funny, I thought, if just like I'm wondering about
his past lives, he were wondering about mine.

Chapter Thirty-eight

Pale Eyes/Pale Triangles

The phone rang. A voice shouted, "Sunshine, it's Jenny, your past from Europe. Remember? We chased castles and dreams together in our student days!"

I hadn't seen Jenny since she and her husband had visited me in Honolulu.

"I'm coming to Phoenix on Friday to see my father. I'd love to drive up to Sedona and see you."

"Could you come one day earlier?" I asked. "I have plans to fly to Honolulu Saturday, but I really want to see you." She said she would.

I'd thought of my upcoming visit to Honolulu as another phase of my healing. I hadn't been there for five years. I was going to stay with my friend Carrie. She called and said she would have a large dinner party while I was there. I was pleased to hear this because there were many people I wanted to see.

Carrie choose her words carefully and said, "Tanya has been asking about you. She wants to see you."

Her words hit me hard. I had long been dreading the day I would see Tanya again, though I was sure it wasn't because I was afraid of her anymore. I knew my own feelings now; I wasn't burying them as I had for so many years. But while my mind was telling me there was nothing in me that wanted to see her again, my heart was beating rapidly.

Was there more for me to learn from knowing Tanya? Hadn't I handled it all?

I knew Carrie was asking me if it would be all right to invite Tanya to the dinner party.

"Yes," I replied, hoping my pause had not given away how shaken I'd become. "I expected to bump into her somewhere anyway, so that would be fine for you to invite her."

That was all Carrie was waiting to hear. She went on, "Good. Tanya asked me to arrange this dinner party so she could see you. I have twelve people coming on the Wednesday after you arrive."

So Tanya hadn't changed at all; she was still acting like the Queen. Maybe that's what I *needed* to know.

I hung up the phone.

I wanted my body to tell me what it was feeling. Was there fear? Was there anticipation? Was there anything?

Mostly I heard the voice in my mind saying, *It's time to wrap it up, time to wrap it up and move on.*

When Jenny arrived, I felt free to tell her about my past lives and all the other things I'd learned through the years of seeing castles, turrets, black boots, and pale green eyes.

I realized clearly that it was no accident that Jenny, the only person in the world who'd known *both* Madison and Tanya, had come to Sedona to visit me only five days before I was to see Tanya in Honolulu.

Jenny listened as I told her all I now knew about Madison, and what had happened to him. Then I told her what the bartender had said. I found that I could talk about most of it with little or no emotion, as if it were a novel I had read, a bad novel at that. I felt like there was nothing left to heal regarding Madison.

As I told Jenny about Tanya, the patterns of control and power were clear: "First I had the power as a monk during the Inquisition. I'd started as this loving, peaceful, woman who had the power to heal. I disguised myself as a monk so I could travel and do my healing more easily. When Tanya, who was the Inquisitor and a control freak, arrested me and started questioning my beliefs, I became enraged. She then found out I was a woman, and began to torture me. I turned my power from light to dark and I wanted to use it to destroy her."

I knew Jenny had been listening very carefully. I saw a puzzled look cross over her face and waited for her question.

"Marilyn, how do you know all this?"

"Jenny, sometimes I did meditations on it or self-hypnotic relaxations. I once even went to Brian Weiss for a hypnotic regression. Do you know when you are hypnotized you at first don't think you're really under—that you're really hypnotized—you just think you're making it all up?"

"No, I didn't know that." Jenny shook her head and I continued.

"Well, it's true. And it takes a while for you to realize that since they're your thoughts—they're coming from you—that you can trust them." I gave Jenny time to let this revelation sink in before I went on.

"But mostly it just happened, it was a *knowing*. I call it the *Aha* moment. One moment you just know something that you didn't know before. It can be blazoned before your mind's eye, your forehead, or your windshield, as happened with many of my visions on how to do a portrait. Does that help to answer your question?"

Jenny nodded that she understood, and I went on.

"So, my desire to misuse power at the Inquisition made me afraid of myself and my power and led me to be powerless in my next life as an artist in the Queen's court. And, of course, Tanya was the Queen and had all the power."

I went on with the details of pink triangled lapels, portraits, and Tanya having me pushed off the turret when I tried to leave her.

"Well, it was really a surprise when I found myself in black boots as a Nazi youth." I saw Jenny's eyes widen and knew she was shocked.

"Jenny," I went on to explain, "all of us have had lifetimes that are hard to face. It's the nature of karma that we have to learn *all* the lessons and strangely, that's the only day in that lifetime I remember." Jenny closed her mouth and I went on, "Maybe it's the only day in that lifetime I needed to live. I've thought about that one a lot. It could be we only need one day—one event from a lifetime to stir up the patterns we need to get in touch with.

"It may be we can actually borrow a day from another person!" I began to laugh. "Can't you imagine it, walking up to someone and saying, 'Excuse me, May I borrow your Tuesday?'" Jenny laughed, too.

"Well, anyway, it's not really that unusual to have only one day. You rarely get chunks of time or daisy fields—instead you get a traumatic event that you have something attached to and that is affecting your life now. It pops up so you can work on it just as you meet the people you've shared other lifetimes with, so you can work out or at least *see* the patterns you've shared. But I'm digressing."

I paused and gave Jenny some time to let all this sink in.

"So there I was as a young soldier in the Nazi Youth," I went on. "When I saw Tanya's pale green eyes in front of me, I knew they looked familiar. She was only a child, but instead of killing her as I had been ordered to do, I dropped my gun and was cradling her in my arms, trying to remember who she was. Then, I was hit in the back by a rifle butt—we both fell into the ditch, and were shot. We died together."

Jenny stared at me. The smile had left her face.

"So you see, by not using the power against her I broke the karmic circle, but I died thinking I had to know whose pale green eyes they were and that I had to continue to protect her.

"So now here I am again," I continued, "only this time I fall in love with a woman so it can really push my buttons and make me question the patterns. Yet even here, I repeat the pattern about having to protect her, and *again* I give up my power, until I finally learned that I had to say goodbye."

Jenny waited for me to take a sip of my coffee before she asked, "So what is it now, Marilyn? Why are you so determined to see her in Honolulu?"

I began to protest that I didn't set it up, she did, but somewhere deep inside I knew I also wanted to see her. I was not sure why. I thought perhaps it was to see how little emotion I had left about any of it.

The night of the party I dressed very carefully as I knew Tanya would. She'd always been an impeccable dresser. In fact, in my co-dependency, I'd often cared more how she'd dressed than how I did.

My new off-white suit made me look light and happy.

Several people arrived at the same time. Tanya was near the back of the group. I heard her voice growing a pitch higher as she moved from one to another, hugging each and saying, "Hello, darling. Hello, darling," in that falsetto voice that almost rang with an accent, and that I remembered so well.

I was busy greeting one after another myself. Then she stood directly in front of me.

Nothing could have prepared me . Even with all those rehearsals in my mind, and asking my angels to be with me, I was not ready for what I saw: Tanya stood there in the *pale pink blouse with the triangle lapel.* It was now a very faded pink. It was almost a grey, grubby pink, but it was unmistakably the same blouse that now had to be more than fifteen years old.

Her face was perched above the triangle. Her prismatic olive-green eyes fixed on me.

"Hello, Tanya, how are you?" I asked, knowing my angels were with me and that I had given no outward sign of my shock at seeing her wearing an old symbol of our relationship.

Her lids narrowed over her ice-green eyes as she said, "Marilyn, how good to see you." She leaned forward to place her cheek against mine and put her arms around my body in a hug, all the while making sure she didn't disturb her hair. How very Tanya—do not disturb the hair!

Sometime during the evening, I had a conversation with Pepper. She seemed to have to sit most of the night. I'd heard she'd been very ill.

"You look well," she said. "I hear wonderful things about you and your paintings traveling everywhere."

"I am, and they are," I replied softly.

I reached forward. I felt compassion for her for I knew *she* was now the one living under Tanya's control. Then I remembered my words to her so long ago for the first time since I had uttered them: "Sometimes I feel so trapped—if only someone could help me, "and I knew that, ironically, that *she* had. I placed my hand gently on her shoulder and said, "Thank you, Pepper, thank you."

She nodded. I saw a sadness enter her eyes and I knew she understood exactly what I meant.

*C*hapter *Thirty-nine*

A Goodbye to Leilani

"And the song, from beginning to end, I found in the heart of a friend."
　　　　　—HENRY WADSWORTH LONGFELLOW
　　　　　The Arrow and the Song

It was early the next morning, too early, but my eyes popped open and words were pouring through my head. Words of a book I never dreamed of writing, but was now begging to be written. A book about four lifetimes.

By eight, when Carrie woke up, I had thirty pages of notes and an outline that involved the first thirteen chapters. I also had a sketch of a pale pink blouse with a triangle lapel so I would never forget what led me to begin this book.

Carrie had planned an outing for that day, but was very understanding when I told her I needed to stay in all day and write.

The following day, I left Carrie's to head for home. I had several hours before my plane was to fly back to Sedona. Remembering how Leilani and I always loved *pikakes leis*, I drove to the downtown lei stand. Makalani was still there, her big brimmed hat, her trademark, covering her thick, salt-and-pepper hair.

"Makalani, I need a four-strand *pikake lei*."

Her chubby, golden fingers picked out a three-strand lei and then she began to carefully weave another strand into the ribboned circle.

"Here, my dear, but why four strands?"

"One for each lifetime," I said matter-of-factly. "And I'm going to share this with Leilani."

Makalani's eyes grew misty and she nodded. Everyone missed Leilani.

I drove to the hillside cemetery where Leilani was buried. I was so sorry I couldn't have Apollo with me, but Hawaii's strict quarantine laws prohibited it. I knew Leilani and Apollo would have liked each other.

I entered the iron gates surrounding the cemetery and drove to Leilani's gravesite.

After draping the four strands over her headstone, I stood back and stared at the message inscribed in small, block letters. Her ex-husband, for once, had done something right.

It read:

SHE WANTED IT ALL
SHE DESERVED IT
SHE ALMOST GOT IT

"Leilani," I said, "I wish I'd known then what I know now—I wish I could have shared it all with you. Remember the little machine I told you I'd built and how it didn't run and how I'd stopped believing? Well, Leilani, I believe again and I could make it run now."

I paused, hoping the tradewinds would bring a message from Leilani. A breeze caught one strand of the *pikake lei* and lifted it away from the others. I watched it, knowing it was a sign that this lifetime of mine had lifted away from the lifetime of the Inquisition, of the castle, and of Nazi Germany. I could tell once again that Leilani was listening and I went on.

"Leilani, *we get what we believe.* You believed the Night Stalkers would get you. You gave your power over to them, just as I gave my power over to Tanya and to my beliefs that I was small and no good. Don't you see, Leilani?" I paused for a long time. "Or are you the one telling me how it really is now? Are these *your* messages to me?"

I threw back my head and laughed. Yes, it was Leilani telling me how to live, how to have it all, how to stop the karmic game of cause and effect.

Karma is a game of the past. It saps tremendous amounts of your energy from the present, the energy that you use for being creative. Creative energy is always in the present, the NOW!

Karma is always of the past and you're always trying to make it right—to do it right. It's like a bad game of Russian roulette: you try it sitting, try it standing, try it over and over, thinking it won't kill you if you do it right. And all the while, all you have to do is stop playing the game to win. *Stop playing the karmic game* of trying to make the past right and walk away from it. Walk away from your past patterns and *live in the now!*

"Leilani, are you telling me I created all these lifetimes with Tanya so I would see I was repeating past patterns of powerlessness and that ultimately, once having seen them, I would drop these patterns? Leilani, did I *create all this pathos—create it so I could get this lesson— so that I could find myself!*"

The gentle breeze stopped and I knew I had my answer. I stood there as an overwhelming feeling of cleansing tingled through my body. I knew I'd never forget all that had happened, but I also knew there was another thing I needed to do. I needed to forgive everyone along my path who had ever done me harm and even more importantly, I needed to forgive myself for my part in it all.

Finally I pulled myself from my reverie—it was time to go catch my plane. I threw one last kiss toward Leilani's headstone and said, "Obviously you have it all now, Leilani. Thanks. Thank you for the messages, thank you for telling me how it is—thanks for being my friend!"

Driving down the hill, words flowed with my tears.

"Mom, you were right. *Love can reach from beyond the grave.*"

Before I drove back to Sedona from the airport in Phoenix, I stopped and bought a computer. I wrote "writer" in the space where it asked for occupation on the warranty slip I filled out.

Then, once back in Sedona, I introduced four-pound Apollo to my four-pound laptop computer and said, "Meet your new little sister, Athena. We will all be doing a lot of traveling together."

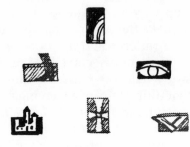

*C*hapter Forty

To Climb a Mountain

Come to the edge, he said.
They said: We are afraid.
Come to the edge, he said.
They came,
He pushed them . . . and they flew.
　　　　　　　　　—GUILLAUME APOLLINAIRE

A few months have passed since that party in Honolulu. I've finally had a child, I've finally been able to give birth: it is this book.

Now I know why I didn't go back to find that castle or the portrait with the pink triangle bodice on my last trip to Europe. I was supposed to see that last triangle on Tanya's pale pink blouse in Honolulu instead.

I was also to realize that I had finally taken back my power when Tanya said to me at the door, "Now you can call me and we can get together."

I'd looked directly into her pale green eyes and said with no malice, no emotion, only telling the truth as I'd promised myself I would do, "No, I won't be doing that." In my mind it was with a hint of sadness that I said, *No, this time we were born to say goodbye.*

When I got back to Sedona and started writing, I thought of Leilani's messages to me as I was standing in the cemetery, and I realized it was not a person we're born to say goodbye to, but our past patterns. That we become lured by and addicted to the familiar, negative or positive, and can become trapped in our patterns of the past. And as long as we are operating out of the past, we are doomed to repeat it.

And so we seek out others who are familiar, look for those we know, as Tanya and I had in so many lives, thinking we can use each other as a way to work out our patterns. But often we only switch roles and just continue to repeat the patterns.

Karma is always a control issue. We think that we must save someone or protect them, or that they must save or protect us. That we must make up for our past indiscretion to them, or they must make it up to us.

And all the while, it continues to sap our energy from the present and we continue to gather more and more debt, more and more karma—good or bad—simply by staying on the wheel, simply by playing the game.

Just like the debt that never gets paid off because you're always accumulating interest that you must pay, even to owing interest on the interest. Or like the game of Russian roulette that you have no way of winning, that you never get right.

Like the message Leilani had blown by me with the tradewinds, you can play the game standing, you can try it sitting, you can constantly change the rules or position of the game, but sooner or later you will have the chamber with the bullet come up. It is a game you will never win by playing it—*so just stop playing the game.* Stop putting the gun to your head and stop pulling the trigger.

The karmic wheel is like that game. You will never get it right, you will never totally stop accumulating karma—good or bad. And it doesn't matter if it *is* good or bad; it is still there as long as you are playing the game, as long as you are running your life out of the past.

Yes, *we are born to say goodbye, to say goodbye to all our past patterns* and forgive everyone and ouselves for our part in it!

We need to stop thinking that how we lived yesterday is the way to live today. We must say goodbye to the familiar and *go to the edge, go into the unknown!* LET EVERY DAY BE ITS OWN DAY, creating each day for its own sake. And let yourself be who you really are, giving up the roles you've assumed and played until you've begun to believe they are you. Give up possessing other people or letting them possess you. Give up the past patterns of fear and war and the limiting beliefs about history repeating itself.

We have the opportunity to do things differently, to believe differently, to *create a new world!* But to do so, we must risk being *present* and *now!* We must start operating out of the *now!* It's only from the *now* that we're truly alive, can be effective and creative, can be *giving* and *loving* and can *BE WHO WE REALLY ARE!*

And once we operate out of *who we are*, we can began to focus on a world of *Love and Peace.*

In the eternity of time, we are a breath away from knowing there is life everywhere. Other worlds are waiting for us to fulfill our destiny and to take our place among the galaxies. To do this, we must go to the edge, to the unknown—jump into the NOW, for only in the now can we create—create a world of Love and Peace.

Go to the edge and jump—and *you may fly!!*

Even though it had been a long day of writing, I stretched and put a new batch of paper into my computer's printer. Words about "how to operate out of the NOW" and "how to be creative" were pouring into my head.

I looked down at Apollo, who was nudging my leg. I knew he was in my life to protect me and keep me on track. His nudging was his way of telling me it had been a long enough day—and a long enough journey—and that this book was finished.

"Okay, okay, let's take that walk," I said as I clipped Apollo's leash to his collar. "Maybe it's time to take a long break—a vacation. When we get back from our walk, I'm going to pack us up—maybe we'll go live in Paris for a while. You'd love Paris—with all its smells, you could spend a whole month on one street corner." Apollo's tail wagged.

"Or maybe it's time to go climb a mountain!"

Afterthought

I began this book with the conviction that the title would be *BORN TO SAY GOODBYE* (which was seen in a vision long before I began to write), and it meant saying goodbye to a particular person. Then, as the book progressed, I grew to think it meant saying goodbye to past patterns and karma.

At the completion of the book, just before going to press, I got another *"Aha!" a knowing:* after living on this planet through many lifetimes, after having been through much pathos as well as joy, after having seen many changes in the Earth's galactic growth, and after growing to love it and many of you, my fellow travelers—I know it is time for me to move on. There are so many other worlds to explore!

And so, with a joy of graduating but also a sadness at saying goodbye, I now know the true meaning is I was BORN TO SAY GOODBYE to planet Earth.

But before I say goodbye, I have several more stories to tell and a few more books to write. My guides are whispering of the next one already.

Epilogue

Be Who You Are
A Journey Into Self-Discovery

This section is offered to show, in brevity and simplicity, an outline of some of the methods I've used on my journey into self-discovery. You might also find these methods useful on your own path.

As you venture into your own discoveries, keep in mind that your *point of power* is the present, the NOW! It is in the *now* that you can be creative and make changes, not in the past.

You cannot look to the past for answers, or you will only repeat your mistakes.

Walk gently and lovingly through life, acting each day with kindness to all others, for we are all on this journey together.

Suggestions for Self-Discovery

- Begin and end each day with gratitude
- Affirm who you are each day
  (come out of your smallness and into your magnificent, unlimited self)
- Acknowledge the life force in all things and carry a reverence for that life
- Get rid of the "shoulds" in your life
- Walk gently and do no harm to others, to the environment, to yourself in thought or in deed
- Wrap the light around yourself for protection
  (do it gently and with flexibility, so you allow the love to flow in and flow out, yet stay impervious to the negative and the dark)
- Begin listening to the small voice that comes from within and then begin to act on its counsel (begin with the simple things and you will develop an inner voice; it will not mislead you as your ego sometimes does)
- Know that forgiving is essential for letting go of "stuff" (forgiving others as well as yourself)
- Always walk with a sense of humor

Methods for Self-Discovery

Dream Interpretation

1) Keep a pad by your bedside. Immediately upon waking, write down your dream. Write rapidly and do not censor what you're writing. (If you have trouble remembering your dreams, try giving yourself the suggestion, before you go to sleep, that you will remember your dreams upon awakening. Give the process time. You will improve.)

2) Go through what you've written and underline any words or phrases that especially strike you or seem to stand out.

3) Take another piece of paper and at the top of the page write:

   • Your mood upon waking
   • Anything that has happened within a few days that may relate to the dream

4) Draw a line down the center of the rest of the page. To the left side of the line, put all the words or phrases you have underlined. Then to the right, and next to each word or phrase, list what they mean to you.

ex.	horn	Gabriel, blowing, news
	red auto	hot, movement, danger
	light	idea, help, hope

After you've finished your list, go back over it to see if any patterns are emerging. (Refer back to the chapter called "Interlude" on pages 32 & 33 and note the symbols for "left leg—what was LEFT").

Practice will decidedly help you with your dream interpretation. Trust your own dreams. They're trying to tell you something.

> **Please note:** Dreams vary greatly. Those that seem more real and are more easily remembered probably have deeper meaning. Simple ones may contain an answer to yesterday's problems, while those shrouded in tremendous symbolism are harder to interpret. These often come from deeper in the subconscious and thus bear deeper messages.
>
> You can also program yourself to get answers to certain problems or situations by making such suggestions to yourself before you go to sleep. You may thus have a dream that will act out an answer or the answer may appear to you sometime during the following day.

DAYDREAMING, MEDITATING, SELF-HYPNOSIS AND PRAYER

I've lumped these methods together because each of them can lead you to an altered state of consciousness. I've personally used each of these methods at one time or another.

DAYDREAMING

My current favorite. I find it immensely creative and very easy to do; in fact, I'm sure none of you needs instructions on how to daydream—only the *permission* and encouragement to do it.

Daydreaming is the least directive of all these methods. All you have to do is let your mind wander. It's also lots of *fun!*

MEDITATION AND SELF-HYPNOSIS

Both acts create a *sustained focus,* unlike daydreaming, which encourages *mind wandering.*

Many common endeavors can act like a meditation or become self-hypnotic. Examples: a long walk, an artistic project, a repeated task.

There are many formal and not-so-formal forms of meditation that you could learn from the particular organization that practices them or from reading about them.

The method I'd like to suggest is simple:

- Find a comfortable space where you'll have no distractions. (You might try sitting or lying down.) Allow about twenty minutes.
- Close your eyes: There is no wrong way to do this, but it's best if you don't use the time to make a mental grocery list.
- Then LISTEN—and take what you get!

Second Method:
For this particular type of meditation, refer to the chapter called "The Flashback" on pages 55 to 57.

1) Think of a physical symptom you'd like to deal with
2) While concentrating on the symptom, go into a deep meditative state
3) Give permission . . . say *yes* or *no* to knowing the truth about it
4) Sit back and let the story unfold

In meditation and in self-hypnosis, you will often think you've made it all up. This also happens in regular hypnosis; in fact, you usually do not believe that you were hypnotized. As time goes by you will learn to trust yourself with self-hypnosis, just as you will learn to trust your own dreams.

I've also gained great benefit from making a tape of my own voice and meditating to it as recommended in Dr. Brian Weiss's book *Through Time Into Healing.*

Note the differences between:

Daydreaming—is mind wandering

Meditation— is listening

Self-Hypnosis—is often more directive

Prayer—is usually directive and requesting

THEY ALL WORK!

Please note: Presently there is a tremendous movement toward professionally-led past-life regressions. This can be exceedingly helpful and can shorten the discovery time, **but,** since the field is growing so rapidly, please choose the regressionist you use with care.

A final type of meditation: TO MEET AN ANGEL OR GUIDE
(We each have at least three angels)
Relax and get ready to go into a directive meditation.

1) Picture yourself climbing a mountain. Note how you feel as you're climbing this mountain: Do you scramble up easily, laboriously pull yourself from rock to rock, walk up lightly or perhaps even float up? This will tell you a lot about yourself and your present mood.
2) Once at the top of the mountain, head across the expanse that lies before you. Is it flat, mountainous, sandy, or watery? Again, this is your journey and it's what *you* see.
3) As you approach the other side of the expanse, you see a building. Enter it. Note the type of building and how you feel now that you've entered it. Now prepare yourself so that when you exit you can meet your angel or guide.
4) Exit the building and walk forward toward the tree to the left. As you approach the tree you see someone coming toward you. Greet that person and ask if he has a message for you. Share with him for a brief while. Thank him and begin to walk back across the expanse. Then return down the mountain.

Thank you. That was your journey—you created it all! **Take what you get!**

Clearing

Clearing is a method that will enable you to release painful and negative emotions that you have attached to a place or an event.

With most such circumstances, there are both negative and positive emotions. The more passionate the emotions, the more likely you will remember one side of the feeling and deny the other. If you deny the negative, it often freezes you into a state of non-growth. Thus, releasing the negative can be most beneficial as it will allow the positive to re-emerge and also allow you to grow and get on with true living.

Refer to chapter 34, pages 189 & 190.

METHOD:

1) Return to a place where an event has happened that was traumatic for you. (You can do this mentally, though sometimes it is most powerful to actually visit the site.)
2) Allow the emotions and pain to resurface.
3) Remain there as long as you need to and until you've exhausted all the pathos. You'll know you've exhausted it all when a small memory of something good or warming or funny begins to enter your thoughts.
4) Allow these good thoughts to rush in.
5) You are cleared and have begun your healing. (You can repeat this method as often as you need to; each time will bring greater healing and clearing).

Apollo had again nudged my leg, telling me I must not forget to tell about another truth of life—that life exists everywhere, in everything, and that it's all from the same source. Just as I respect the consciousness and life in him, I must hold sacred the consciousness and life in all else.

When I sincerely look at him and recognize the reverence of the life in him, I can often pick up his thoughts and I know, with his unconditional love for me, that he even more often reads my thoughts.

THE PATH

There is a path for each of us . . .
It leads to home.
"How will I know when I am on it?
You will know . . . it will feel like going home.
"When will I arrive?"
There is no arrival,
there is the wondrous journey.
And now you know,
   you do not journey alone.